"*We the Pizza* speaks to [...]
successful businesses [...]
trailblazing cookbook, N[...]
and valuable contributi[...]
at reducing recidivism rates among the formerly incarcerated,
this visionary leader serves up fantastic square pies with a side of
African American history and advocacy. *We the Pizza* gives voice
to the new wave of social entrepreneurs honoring the resilience
and strength of our ancestors by embracing our foodways while
pushing them forward."

—TONI TIPTON-MARTIN, James Beard Award–winning author of
Jubilee: Recipes from Two Centuries of African American Cooking and
*Juke Joints, Jazz Clubs, and Juice: Cocktails from Two Centuries of
African American Cookbooks*

"*We the Pizza* is a master class in flavor and purpose, blending
culinary creativity with powerful storytelling to uplift the
community. This is more than a collection of recipes; it's a
blueprint for using food as a force for good."

—JON GRAY, CEO and cofounder of Ghetto Gastro

"In a very crowded pizza book universe, just when it seemed
there was nothing new to be said on the subject, I was thrilled
and delighted to discover Muhammad Abdul-Hadi's *We the
Pizza.* This book reaffirms my hope that the realm of visionary,
inventive, and staggeringly great pizzas will continue to expand
with delicious ferment, while also proving that pizza is indeed
the perfect vehicle for and metaphor of transformation, not
only of ingredients but of people's souls. This book is the story
of that transformation."

—PETER REINHART, author of *Pizza Quest: My Never-Ending Search
for the Perfect Pizza*

"*We the Pizza* is a brilliant depiction of all things that inspire my
career and love of food—a source of community, culture, and
power. Muhammad has brilliantly captured all of the above and
then some."

—STEPHEN SATTERFIELD, award-winning food writer, founder of
Whetstone media, and host of Netflix's *High on the Hog*

WB

THE

PIZZA

SLANGIN' PIES + SAVIN' LIVES

WE THE PIZZA

AWARD-WINNING PIZZA (AND MORE) + STORIES OF SECOND CHANCES FROM PHILADELPHIA'S DOWN NORTH PIZZA

MUHAMMAD ABDUL-HADI

RECIPES BY MICHAEL CARTER, WITH DAVID JOACHIM
PHOTOGRAPHS BY AMURRI LAUREN

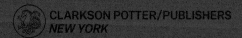
CLARKSON POTTER/PUBLISHERS
NEW YORK

 CONTENTS

FLIP SIDE: Beef bacon + caramelized pineapple + jalapeños + Flip Side BBQ Sauce **108**

Vegan Flip Side 109

SAY YES: Jerk turkey sausage + roasted butternut squash + kale + ricotta + lemon-honey drizzle **110**

MY PART OF TOWN: Shaved beef + caramelized onion + Wiz Sauce **114**

Lehigh Valley Cheesesteak Pizza 115

TALES OF A HUSTLER: Berbere-spiced smoked brisket + Pikliz + Harissa Cheese Sauce **117**

CROSS THE BORDER: Taco-seasoned beef + onions + poblano chiles + tomatoes + lettuce **120**

A LONG WALK: Roasted chicken + roasted red peppers + Basil-Pesto Cream Sauce **122**

SAUCE IT UP: Pickle-brined chicken + spicy pickles + Quick Thai Red Curry Sauce + cilantro **124**

CHOPPED PIZZA: Spicy coconut-braised chicken + red onion + lime + cilantro **126**

GLAMOROUS LIFE: Crab meat + butterflied shrimp + kale chips + Garlic-Parm Sauce + Not Vodka Sauce **128**

WHAT YA LIFE LIKE: Ramen-Cheez-It crust + kippered beef steak + summer sausage + Cheez Wiz + BBQ salsa **133**

PIZZA COLLABS

Beef Shank Ragù, Smoked Scamorza, and Horseradish Pizza: **MARC VETRI 144**

Harissa Chicken Schnitzel Pizza:
MICHAEL SOLOMONOV 148

Vegan Buffalo Mushroom Pizza:
SHENARRI FREEMAN 152

Cheesy Vegan Buffalo Mushroom Pizza **153**

Doro Wat Pizza: **MARCUS SAMUELSSON 155**

Pali Cali Pizza: **REEM ASSIL 158**

Raw and Uncut: **NICOLE AND MICHAEL NICHOLAS 160**

WINGS + FRIES

NORFFALO WINGS 170

BBQ Wings 173

Honey Chipotle Wings 173

Garlic Parmesan Wings 173

Thai Chili Wings 173

VEGAN NORFFALO CAULIFLOWER WINGS 174

Vegan Thai Chili Cauliflower Wings 175

Vegan Za'atar Cauliflower Wings 175

NORF FRIES 176

Spicy Cheese Fries 178

Spicy Crab Fries 178

VEGAN WIZ FRIES 180

Vegan Everything Fries 182

Vegan Spicy Crab Fries 182

LEMONADES + MILKSHAKES

CLASSIC LEMONADE 190

STRAWBERRY LEMONADE 191

BLUEBERRY LEMONADE 194

CUCUMBER-MINT LEMONADE 195

WATERMELON LEMONADE 198

VANILLA MILKSHAKE 201

Vegan Vanilla Milkshake 202

Strawberry Milkshake 202

Oreo Milkshake 202

Apple Pie Milkshake 202

Bean Pie Milkshake 202

FOREWORD

DANNY TREJO, actor, author, restaurateur

When I was a kid, my uncles and my dad would set up a big table of cold cuts and potato salad—it was a time for friends and family, for everyone, to get together and eat. Food has the remarkable ability to unite and transform. It's what I've set out to achieve with my restaurants and tacos. It is what Muhammad has, too, through his personal style of pizza.

As someone who has navigated his share of challenges, I see a lot of myself in Muhammad's story and mission. I'm honored to introduce his cookbook, which contains not only deliciously mouthwatering recipes— some of the juiciest photos I've seen—but also powerful, resilient stories of those impacted by the criminal legal system.

Muhammad understands firsthand the power of second chances. His transition from facing twenty-one felony charges to becoming a beacon of hope for the incarcerated is nothing short of inspiring. Like Muhammad, I've faced my fair share of obstacles. Falling into a life of crime and addiction at a young age led to

multiple incarcerations. I thank God every day for helping me turn my life around and giving me this platform to offer second chances to others and help change their lives— just as Muhammad does with Down North Pizza.

Down North Pizza unites people and transforms lives.

Muhammad's dedication to his mission and craft, even when faced with the darkest times, accompanied by Executive Chef Mike Carter's resilience and determination, are the lifeblood of the restaurant and the spirit behind their pizza. Both are embodied in this cookbook's savory recipes, from out-of-this-world pizza like the I'm a Boss to tasty Norffalo wings—that Norf Sauce is one of a kind.

Thank you, Muhammad, for giving hope to those without it, for exclusively employing the formerly incarcerated, and for pursuing the mission to reduce recidivism rates.

Every recipe is exciting and refreshing. But you don't have to take my word for it. Huddle up with your family and friends and go find out for yourselves.

Down North Pizza unites people and transforms lives.

PREFACE PIZZA DE RESISTANCE

AJIMA OLAGHERE, PhD

This cookbook and the source of its inspiration, Down North Pizza, embody the creative spirit and strivings necessary for transformative change. The ambition, audacity, and sweat equity of the Down North Pizza crew have forged a social-entrepreneurial enterprise to stem the tide of carceral system philosophy, policies, and actions. It starts with a basic nurturance we all need: food; sustenance; literally, "slinging pies to save lives." Down North Pizza manifests our greatest work: the liberation of Black people. This book is a testament to the creative output Black people give birth to, time and again, in the midst of oppressive machinations. This book is a culinary ode to Black people—for us to always think free, be free, love free, eat well, and be well. As you read, flip, and cook your way through these pages, remember it's not just a cookbook but also a movement for liberation—not unlike the work of our ancestors whose lessons echo through time.

As of 2022, the United States holds 1.23 million people in state and federal institutions. When we consider the number of individuals in jail, this total rises to 1.89 million people, and it balloons to 5.63 million people[1] when we include those under some form of state supervision. These grim statistics invite us to envision ways to dismantle mass incarceration and mass supervision. 5.63 million represents not only the number of people incarcerated but also their undeveloped, untapped human potential. 5.63 also reminds us of the persistent equity challenge before us, particularly for minoritized and racialized individuals for whom the carceral system is a dubious mechanism for justice.

Dismantling the prison-supervision industrial complex requires creativity and social-entrepreneurial spirit. It is against this backdrop where the story of Down North Pizza begins. Down North's resistance to the carceral system and its logic extends as far back as the 1600s. From lynching Black bodies and linking Black motherhood to slavery, to the unkept promise of reparations and "40 acres and a mule"; from the exploitation economics of sharecropping and the racist backlash of Black codes, to the hopes, aspirations, and generational wealth deferred because of racial terror and violence; from the political mobilization, resistance, and hope in Fannie Lou Hamer, Malcolm X, and the Black Panther Party's 10-point plan, to present-day abolition and food-sovereignty movements, Down North Pizza emerges with its mission: to heal, and to eliminate the pernicious growth of the carceral state and its many entanglements.

As of 2022, the United States holds 1.23 million people in state and federal institutions.

INTRODUCTION

GRAND OPENING CHAOS

One in every three American Black men my age goes to prison. I went to college, and I studied criminal justice. I owned businesses. My ultimate goal was to help Black people be free.

I used to run a record label. I owned a used car lot and autobody shop. I operated a thriving network of thirteen addiction-recovery houses throughout Pennsylvania, New Jersey, and Delaware. And I had a flourishing real estate business. As a very successful and very serial entrepreneur, I owned the dilapidated building at 28th and Lehigh Streets, in Philadelphia, for five years before bringing it to life as my greatest success (so far): Down North Pizza. Not many people know that during the pizza shop's grand opening, I wore an ankle monitor and kept it plugged into the wall socket near the deep fryer to keep it charged.

That ankle monitor is one reason why Down North Pizza exclusively employs formerly incarcerated people. Employment is a big part of its mission to provide culinary career opportunities at a fair wage in an equitable workplace. But providing jobs is only the beginning. To fully understand what we've done and how we've done it, you need to understand *why* we did it. That story begins before we opened.

While Down North was taking shape, I knew about justice, and I knew about jobs. I did not know about pizza or restaurants. Despite that, in 2018, I spent $250,000 of my own money to build a pizza restaurant with no prior experience in the culinary field and no guidance from others. I went through all the byzantine inspections, permits, licenses, and paperwork to get a restaurant open in the city of Philadelphia. With the help and support of my wife and three kids, I also earned my B.A. in Criminal Justice from Temple University. I knew this pizza shop would work. The mission is what drove me forward.

The plan was to exclusively hire formerly incarcerated people, give them support, and train them for culinary jobs. This kind of pizza shop would help fulfill my lifelong goal of bringing down the recidivism rates in the city. All of my education and most of my entrepreneurship was aimed at helping to keep underprivileged people off the streets and out of jail. I knew in my soul this pizza shop could be the way.

What I did not yet realize was how much value, wisdom, genius, and innovation there was in the streets themselves. You can give someone a job, but you can't give them their humanity. All you can do is acknowledge it or deny it. In my efforts to provide formerly incarcerated people with jobs, I was reminded that my community is undeniably beautiful in spite of what the system has taken from us. *We the Pizza* is about our glorious journey and just how far we can go together.

SLANGIN' PIES + SAVIN' LIVES

In early 2019, Down North Pizza started getting real. I brought on an up-and-coming Philly chef to run the kitchen (let's call him "Chef E" because things didn't work out in the end). Then, that March, I was hit with a federal indictment involving the addiction treatment center that was contracting my recovery-house company. Up to that point, I had managed to escape the carceral system for thirty-three years. My criminal record was nonexistent, which is an accomplishment for a Black man living in inner city Philadelphia. For doing business with the wrong people, I got indicted on twenty-one felony charges and faced up to twenty years in federal prison, with five years' probation, and potentially had

One in three American Black men my age will go to prison in their lifetime.

to pay $1.5 million in restitution. (Read the details on page 138.)

That indictment only served to make me more determined to get Down North open.

The slowness of the legal system, which usually crushes lives under the weight of hearings, filings, and continuances, worked to my advantage. Various postponements, including the 2020 Covid-19 pandemic lockdowns, delayed my trial for months. I awaited trial for an entire year, during which time I continued working on the pizza shop. My trial came in June 2020. After the judgment, I had to close my network of addiction-recovery houses, I lost my car dealer's license, and I couldn't pursue new business licenses because I now had a conviction. I went on house arrest that summer, could work only limited hours, and had to wear an ankle monitor. But I still kept renovating the shop, hiring staff, and developing the restaurant menu. We started doing pizza popups in the fall of 2020 to test out the menu and the Down North concept, and the response was overwhelmingly positive. It was slow, hard work building a restaurant business while on house arrest, but there was no way I was going to stop. By the time we did the popups, I had enough experience with the carceral system to know that this pizza shop—and its mission— had to succeed.

Everyone on the Down North staff has been imprisoned, including me (house arrest is a form of incarceration). We give people good jobs, fair wages, legal support if they need it, and in some cases, even a place to live rent-free for six months in a government-subsidized apartment right upstairs over the shop.

Our Philly spin on Detroit-style pizza is what makes it all possible. Our executive chef, Mike Carter, spent two whole years getting it perfect, while I was dealing with my indictment (more about Mike—and our pizza—on page 60). By the time we finally had Down North's Grand Opening, on March 19, 2021, our pizzas were dialed in and tasted amazing. People couldn't get enough of 'em.

Thanks to some good word of mouth from the popups, a little social media, and a few positive local news stories, the community was primed for us to open.

On opening weekend, we got slammed with orders, we were understaffed, and we quickly ran out of supplies, but Mike was—and still is—a beast. He is a master at catering, a talent he picked up while running the kitchen at Greensburg State Correctional Institution, in upstate Pennsylvania. Prison work isn't something that ends up on your résumé, but Mike learned some valuable skills, and every pizza he turns out is a thing of beauty. The crust is super-crunchy outside and airy inside. The cheese blend (mozzarella, provolone, and cheddar) browns up all lacy and crispy along the edges. And he spoons our signature smoky-sweet-hot Norf Sauce (page 34) over the top. Where Mike's creativity really shines is in the toppings, like lamb sausage with za'atar and lemon ricotta (see page 104) and berbere-spiced smoked brisket with Harissa Cheese Sauce and Pikliz (see page 117)—some people call it the best Detroit-style pizza outside of the Motor City. I'd like to take that one step further and call it the best and most inventive pizza you'll ever taste.

During opening weekend, I didn't touch a single pie. Back then, I didn't even know how to hold a knife, and I definitely wasn't expecting to be in the kitchen that day. But from the moment we opened, we had hundreds of orders coming in, both online and in person, and I was needed. "Just keep droppin' wings and fries," they shouted out as I manned the fryer. (I used the wall socket near the fryer to keep my ankle monitor charged.) Mike was throwing down on the pizza build and the bake. Chef E was out front, finishing and expediting. That was our assembly line. This was one of the biggest days of our lives. We had hundreds of orders for pizzas, wings, fries, and shakes—and there were only three of us in the kitchen.

From an operations standpoint, it was a disaster. Not only were we short-staffed, short on raw ingredients, and even short on pizza pans, but also just before we opened the top oven had broken!

You better believe that Mike didn't miss a beat. He turned that top oven into a proofing box for the dough to speed up production. Mike was deep in the pocket—going back and forth from the build to the bake, and then down to the basement for more dough.

From the moment we opened on noon that Saturday, until we closed late that Sunday night, the three of us were rockin' nonstop. Even when the shop was closed, we were cranking out dough, prepping toppings, and stirring up Norf Sauce.

All weekend long, people lined up down the block and past the library to 29th Street, waiting to get one of our pizzas. We also had stacks of tickets from Tock, our online ordering app, and we didn't set a limit on how many pies people could order on the app (rookie mistake). Before we even cracked open the door on that first day, we had 100 pies already sold. The people in line didn't know why other people were just walking up and collecting their pizzas. There was hella confusion, but we made it happen.

Mike was building a dozen pies at a time, going like mad. He had to squat down every time he opened the bottom oven. At one point, he looked at me and said, "As a kid, I was the catcher on the baseball field." I didn't know what he meant; he smiled that big contagious smile and added, "I was built for squats." We laughed, but after squatting all day, and running up and down those basement stairs to cut the dough, his legs locked up that night. He had to get a leg massage before he could start work the next day.

On Day 2, we ran out of dough. Mike had to mix and proof a batch super fast. We were scrambling to keep up. Plus, the three of us had phone messages coming in all day. The media were calling from all over. And family was stopping by, wanting to say hello and congratulate us. They would text and say, "Hey, can you come outside?" If we managed to catch a break, we'd leave the kitchen for a hot minute, kiss some babies and smile for selfies, then run right back into the kitchen to sling more pies.

Roc the Mic (page 94), a pepperoni pizza, was our biggest seller. It still is. But Mike's a chef, so he was putting people onto cool combos like What We Do (page 96), our meat lover's pie with beef pepperoni, beef sausage, sautéed kale, pickled banana peppers, and Honey Chipotle Sauce. Or, Yeah That's Us (page 100), our spicy buffalo chicken pizza. (You might be wondering, *What's up with these pizza names?* All our pies are named for Philly rap songs. Because . . . yeah, that's what we do. And if you didn't notice, the menu is halal, too.)

IN THIS TOGETHER

Out on the street, the block was hot. We had all these red and white balloons, and a local DJ was laying down a party vibe. Thanks to some key contacts, the Philadelphia 76ers basketball team sent us Franklin the Dog, their mascot, to cheer us on. Drummers were on the street hyping up the long line of hungry people. Things were poppin' and because the news crews had gotten wind of us during the pizza popups, the media were all over it.

When I did manage to step outside for a minute, everything I had dealt with during the past five years to get Down North open suddenly flashed before me like a movie trailer. I may have been smiling and shaking hands on the outside, but inside I was reliving my indictment and seeing my face all over the news for all the wrong reasons. I was seeing things as they were the year before, when 2804 West Lehigh was a shell of a building on a beat-up street. I saw us busting up the concrete to install new plumbing to bring the place up to code. I saw the mountains of paperwork: applications for variances to be permitted as a restaurant, the architect's drawings showing the layout for the sink, stoves, and cooking equipment, deciphering the voltages and electric loads we'd be dealing with, documenting our pest-control protocol, determining the dumpster and compost locations, writing the employee handbook, and fighting the city when they tried to say we had to install fire safety sprinklers on every floor of the building.

Not to mention everything that went down with staffing to get the pizza shop open. I was not then and am still not a chef, so I needed someone to handle all things culinary. I mean *everything*. When we started, I didn't know anything about cooking or restaurants; I just knew how to run a business. Then, a week before the grand opening, Chef E tells me he's having trouble finding formerly incarcerated cooks. He says, "I'm gonna have to get some other cooks in here." He was suggesting that we change the restaurant's mission, but I told him straight up: "Absolutely not." The mission is the reason this business exists. I would rather not open Down North than change the mission. I told him, "Figure it out." But he didn't hire anyone, and that's why we were so screwed on opening weekend.

To this day, I don't know how we made it through the opening. The three of us turned out more than 1,000 pizzas—ten different kinds, including a few vegan ones, plus four kinds of chicken wings, four kinds of hand-cut fries, four different lemonades, and some milkshakes. Inside, the kitchen was a train wreck, but from the outside, the place was a success. Everyone loved the food, the vibe, and the mission. The media, the customers, and the community came together over some fantastic pizza—and they got to see that formerly incarcerated people are just like you and me.

Over the next couple months, it was inevitable that someone in the Down North kitchen would spot my ankle monitor. That's when the staff found out that even the boss was on probation. I hadn't made a big deal of it because I didn't want that to be the lead story about Down North—the owner got arrested in an insurance fraud case. No, I wanted to keep the vibes high, both inside the shop and out. But when they saw the ankle monitor, the staff realized I was like them. That ended up validating all the work we were doing. It bonded us tighter as humans, and it connected the dots between the restaurant's mission and the people making it happen.

The truth is that most formerly incarcerated people want to make things right. We are people who have valuable skills. We are people who want good jobs, we are people with families. We love, feel pain, and want to be productive in our communities. Just because someone got convicted of a crime doesn't mean they are a bad person. A lot of people are wrongfully convicted. A lot of innocent people get put away.

One-third of the U.S. population has had some kind of run-in with the country's incarceration system. That's 110 million citizens. Something's seriously wrong with that number. One of the biggest tragedies occurs when young people get locked up because they made a dumb mistake with drugs or got in with the wrong crowd. Usually that happens because they had limited opportunities due to their socioeconomic situation. Then a few years later, they wise up, but they might still be in prison, serving time for a stupid mistake they made when they were just a kid. A lot of these people never get the chance to make things right. And if and when they do get out, they have to survive with the stigma. They have to explain their mistakes in every job interview. And in a bunch of states around the country, they are barred from ever voting in political elections.

At Down North, we give formerly incarcerated people a second chance. We offer people an opportunity to show the world their worth, a chance to be in a positive work environment and make some of the best pizzas you'll ever taste. It's a chance to be a part of something that benefits the community. In this book, Down North staffers also get a chance to tell their personal stories. These are stories of how they grew up and the food they love; how they got on the wrong side of the law; how they did their time; and then, how they turned their lives around with the help of a pizza shop.

These people are not statistics. They are real, live, breathing, bleeding people. They are people who deserve as much love, encouragement, and opportunity as anybody else. Down North is our doorway to that better future.

—MUHAMMAD ABDUL-HADI,
founder, Down North Pizza

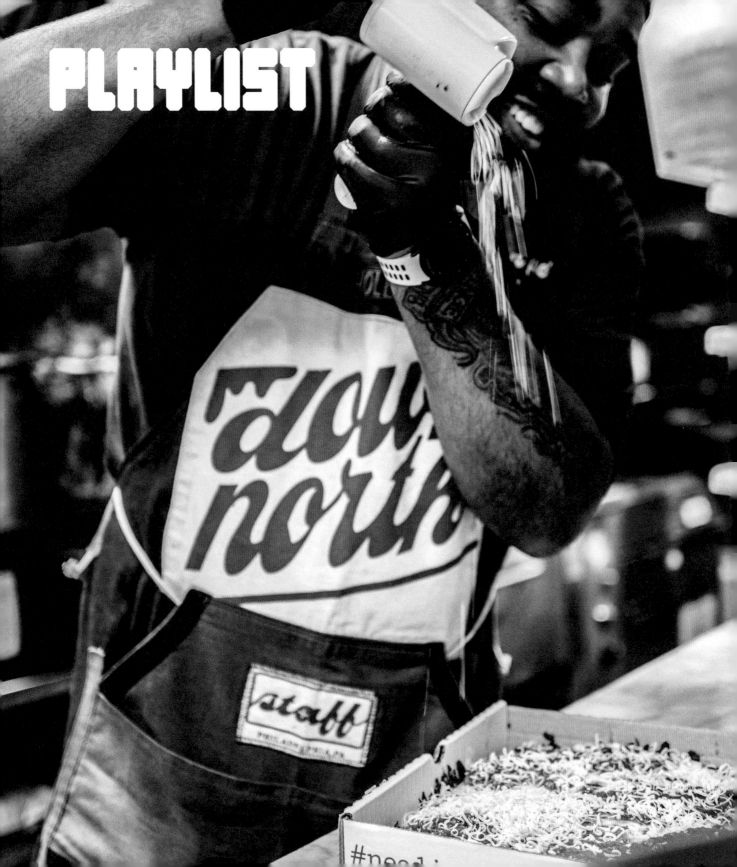

When you walk into the pizza shop Down North, one of the first things you notice is the music. We play all kinds of songs but mostly hip-hop. And we give Philly lots of love. So much good music has come out of this city that we name every one of our pizzas after a song by a Philadelphia musical artist. Here's the full playlist with notes on how the song inspired the pizza. To hear these songs on Spotify, scan the QR code.

VEGETABLE & VEGAN PIZZAS

"NO BETTER LOVE" BY YOUNG GUNZ 64

Our plain cheese pizza is simple and perfect, just like this song by Young Chris and Neef Buck. These two guys got signed to Roc-A-Fella Records in the 2000s, and "No Better Love" appeared on their 2004 album, *Tough Luv*. It's a Philly classic just like this pie.

"UPTOWN VIBES" BY MEEK MILL 66

When we first created the Uptown Vibes veggie pizza in the fall of 2020, Meek Mill's "Uptown Vibes" was poppin' in the club. With that trap, reggaeton, and hip-hop mix, it reminded us of this pie; a mix of peppers, onions, kale, and mushrooms.

"P.S.K. WHAT DOES IT MEAN" BY SCHOOLLY D 68

P.S.K. (Park Side Killers) is considered the first-ever gangsta rap song. Schoolly D was rapping about a park we all knew in Philly. We made the connect with the park being green and vegans being green. Boom—there was the name for our vegan cheesesteak pizza.

"SUMMERTIME" BY DJ JAZZY JEFF & THE FRESH PRINCE 70

If you don't know this Will Smith song, roll down your windows on a hot day, crank up the bass, and soak in the classic Philly vibes with a warm slice of this pizza. Pan-roasted tomatoes, basil pesto, and roasted red peppers taste like this song sounds.

"TWOFIFTEEN" BY BLACK THOUGHT 74

"Yo, the big wheel keep turnin' like Ike's and Anna Mae's; The church kitchen hustlin' dinners every Saturday; Pull over, let me grab a plate, I tend to gravitate; Towards how fish dinners from a Styrofoam platter taste." Those opening bars from Black Thought get us every time. He's the frontman for The Roots, the Philly group that hit it big as Jimmy Fallon's house band on *The Tonight Show*. With this song, Black Thought immortalized Philly's area code, 215. And our Twofifteen pizza is our way of immortalizing another Philly signature: the city's classic roast pork sandwich with broccoli rabe and sharp provolone.

"SARA SMILE" BY HALL & OATES 78

When we made a special vegan pastrami pizza for Down North, the flavors worked so perfectly, they reminded us of that easy-listening song, "Sara Smile," by Philly's classic hitmakers, Hall & Oates.

"STREETS OF PHILADELPHIA" BY BRUCE SPRINGSTEEN 84

We came up with a potato, leek, and bacon pizza for Triple Bottom Brewing, one of our favorite breweries in the city. When we served it at the brewery, the crowd seemed like they were Bruce Springsteen fans, so we called the pizza Streets of Philadelphia. That song, the video, and the movie capture the City of Brotherly Love in a way that's hard to explain.

MEAT & SEAFOOD PIZZAS

"ROC THE MIC" BY BEANIE SIGEL AND FREEWAY 94

Jay-Z opened up his Roc-A-Fella Records label to other artists in the early 2000s. Soon after that, this song became one of the label's big hits, a slam dunk party rap you could always count on. Just like our Roc the Mic pepperoni pizza.

"WHAT WE DO" BY FREEWAY, JAY-Z, AND BEANIE SIGEL 96

"If my kids hungry, snatch the dishes out ya kitchen; I'll be wilding 'til they pick me out a line-up; Even though what we do is wrong . . . Still deliver the order, man; And I ain't talking 'bout chicken and gravy, man." These lines from "What We Do" always hit home for us. And they speak to the spirit of our meat lover's pizza. We don't serve pork at Down North, so our meat lover's pie is topped with halal beef sausage, halal beef pepperoni, pickled banana peppers, kale, and Honey Chipotle Sauce. That's what we do.

"YEAH THAT'S US" BY MAJOR FIGGAS 100

In the early 2000s, there were two big hip-hop groups in Philly: State Property and Major Figgas. Muhammad knows Wallo from Major Figgas, and we always knew we'd name one of our pies for them. Wallo, Gillie da Kid, Ab Liva, and everyone affiliated with Major Figgas has come into Down North and fucked up a few slices of this buffalo chicken pizza.

"BIG HEAD" BY MS. JADE 103

This was a big hit in the early 2000s for Philly rapper Ms. Jade. Her bars hit us every time, "Cause I stack cheese cheese; I'm whatever it's gonna be be; Uh, and it's all to the good; Never been Hollywood cause I stand for the hood." Her chorus "Get your big head on the floor" just makes you want to get up and dance. That's exactly how we felt when we first tasted this BBQ chicken pizza.

"BREAK YOU OFF" BY THE ROOTS 104

Who does Philly proud? The Roots do. Longtime *Tonight Show* house band. Grammy Award winners. NAACP Award winners. First hip-hop group to storm the stage at Lincoln Center. We're as proud of the Roots as we are of this pie, our jerk lamb sausage white pizza with za'atar and roasted garlic honey drizzle.

"I'M A BOSS" BY MEEK MILL 106

Mike was serving time upstate when this song came up around 2011. At the time, Philly wasn't really making any noise in the hip-hop world. Then we saw the video for this song with Meek Mill and Rick Ross riding dirt bikes through the city. Putting Philly culture on display. When you hear that rap, it makes you puff out your chest. "I'm a Boss . . . I call the shots." Makes you feel like you can do whatever you want. Just like the call we made for our turkey lover's pizza with turkey sausage, turkey pepperoni, mushrooms, and peppers.

"FLIPSIDE" BY PEEDI CRAKK 108

This song had Philly in the cobra clutch when it came out in 2003. It was Peedi Crakk's introduction to the rap scene, and it's a straight-up block-party banger. Just like this caramelized pineapple, pickled jalapeño, and beef bacon BBQ pizza. Like Peedi raps in the song, "Yes, this is Philly, you welcome to come check us."

"SAY YES" BY FLOETRY 110

Before Mike came on as the executive chef of Down North, he made a sort-of trial pizza to see if he'd get the job. This Floetry song was floatin' in his mind, "All you got to do is say yes . . . Open up your mind and just rest." His trial pizza, with jerk turkey sausage, butternut squash, kale, and ricotta was a solid hit. Everyone said Yes, and he got the job.

"MY PART OF TOWN" BY TUFF CREW 114

Tuff Crew were one of the groundbreaking Philly groups in early hip-hop. Our guy, Dee, he grew up with the Tuff Crew. He mentioned to them that we got a cheesesteak pizza named after their song, and one of them came through the shop to taste it. That's Philly love right there.

"TALES OF A HUSTLER" BY BEANIE SIGEL 117

This song resonates with a lot of us who grew up in the streets. Like Beanie Sigel says, street life is "just the life we live," and after one of your friends dies, you still got to keep keepin' on. During the pandemic, when Mike started hustling smoked brisket to make ends meet, this song was always in the back of his mind. When he created a smoked brisket pizza with spicy harissa cheese sauce and pikliz Haitian pickles for Down North, this was the only name we could give it.

"CROSS THE BORDER" BY PHILLY'S MOST WANTED 120

When we opened the shop, we had to trim our menu. This beef and cheddar taco pizza with roasted poblanos and cumin sour cream didn't make the cut. But it's so good, maybe we'll bring it back for Cinco de Mayo. Make it a big party and crank up "Cross the Border" by Philly's Most Wanted. Gotta cross the border to get all the cheddar.

"A LONG WALK" BY JILL SCOTT 122

"Your background, it ain't squeaky clean, shit; Sometimes we all got to swim upstream." That lyric in this soulful song makes us feel seen. It's like Jill Scott is saying she's open to being in a relationship with someone who doesn't have the same upbringing as, like, a Ken doll. Yeah Ms. Scott, you got that right. Even formerly incarcerated people can be tender and loving. Her romantic song reminds us of our creamy pesto chicken and roasted pepper pizza. This flavor combo is just so easy to fall in love with.

"SAUCE IT UP" BY LIL UZI VERT 124

Lil Uzi Vert is a Philly rapper we don't listen to much. But he's behind a famous dance move, a kind of shoulder roll, and when you hear his song "Sauce It Up," it just makes you want to roll with it. We had to give Lil Uzi a pizza, and our spicy Thai red curry chicken pie is it.

"GLAMOROUS LIFE" BY COOL C 128

In the early '90s, "Glamorous Life" by Cool C was one of the first major hits out of Philly. Cool C is from Mike's neighborhood, and he's been on death row since 1996. That fact makes this a very special pizza for us. With lump crabmeat, fried shrimp, garlic parmesan sauce, and "not vodka sauce," eating a slice of this pizza feels like living the glamorous life.

"WHAT YA LIFE LIKE" BY BEANIE SIGEL 133

You want to know what life is like in prison? This jailhouse pizza is just a taste. For more, listen to Beanie Sigel's rap on "What Ya Life Like." You'll get the whole platter.

THE DOWN NORTH COMMISSARY

People call Down North pizza Detroit style, but it's really Philly style. We use a different dough than classic Detroit style, our own cheese mix, and unique toppings that tell a story about Philadelphia. We decided on this style of pizza 'cuz it has a special place in our hearts. Everybody in North Philly knows those rectangle slices with the stretchy cheese, whether it's from after school on Fridays or from home when you pull the Ellio's pizza outta the freezer and toss it in the toaster oven. On special occasions, we even had that kind of pizza in the penitentiary. Everybody would spin the line, trying to eat twice on those days! Pizza's just one of those feel-good foods.

Traditional Detroit-style pies are baked in rectangular metal pans and are topped with Wisconsin brick cheese that's pushed to the edges of the pan to create a crispy cheese crust throughout. We also push our cheese to the edge to get that kind of crust, but we use square pans, and we swap out the brick cheese for a Philly-special play of mozzarella, provolone, and cheddar. We often sprinkle parmesan on top to make it a four-cheese pizza.

We use a lighter, fluffier pizza dough, too (see page 30). It's more hydrated than your typical Detroit-style dough. And instead of a basic tomato sauce, we make our signature smoky, sweet, and spicy Norf Sauce (page 34). For the crowning touch, our toppings are unique. Sure, we have plain and pepperoni (we'd be out of business if we didn't!), but we call those pies No Betta Love (page 64) and Roc the Mic (page 94). We also make our Break You Off pizza (page 104), a mix of homemade lamb sausage, lemon ricotta, and za'atar with a roasted garlic honey drizzle. We serve up Big Head (page 103), a BBQ chicken pizza with pepperoncini and red onions. What We Do (page 96) is a meat lover's pizza with beef pepperoni, beef sausage, kale, and banana peppers, plus a Honey Chipotle drizzle. We have dozens more, too. Notice that there's no pork in our toppings. Down North is a halal pizza shop; that's because a big part of our North Philly community is Muslim.

What's with the pizza names? All our pies are named after Philly rap songs. We want to show our local artists some love; that's part of our community vibe. We shout out all kinds of Philly rappers, like Will Smith, Meek Mill, Schooly D, Lil Uzi Vert, Beanie Sigel, Young Gunz, State Property, Major Figgas, Ms. Jade, and The Roots. (Check out all the artists in our musical "playlist" on page 16.) We never would have started this jawn if our community wasn't part of it—our pizza shop serves pies by the people, for the people. BTW, *jawn* is Philly slang for "thing." That is, sometimes we say "jawn" instead of saying the thing's proper name. Like, if you want to mix and match our toppings to create your own jawn, that's totally your call. Have at it.

As formerly incarcerated people ourselves, we're also 100 percent committed to our mission of reducing recidivism rates in our community and around the country. That's why we have included some info about the U.S. incarceration system throughout this book. Prison system reform is a thorny topic. If you're interested, you can enjoy your pizza with a side of history, highlighting American prisons and their connection to slavery and racial disparities that continue to this day.

If you're just here for the food, maybe you have a specific question about the recipes in this book—like, where do we get our halal beef pepperoni? What kind of vegan cheese do we use? What kind of oven and pizza pan do we use? All is revealed next . . .

INGREDIENTS

AJI AMARILLO PEPPER PASTE

Aji amarillo is a yellow-orange chile from Peru. It has a bright, floral flavor and a nice punch of heat. We use Goya yellow pepper paste for the drizzle on our P.S.K. Pizza (page 68). Lots of stores carry it.

BACON

Midamar thick-sliced halal beef bacon is our go-to. Any thick-sliced bacon will work.

BROTH

If you're vegan or vegetarian, Better Than Bouillon makes a good No-Chicken Base that tastes similar to commercial chicken broth. You can use it wherever chicken broth or stock is called for.

CHEESE

The Down North three-cheese blend is shredded mozzarella (low-moisture, whole-milk), provolone, and sharp white cheddar cheeses. When we use parmesan, it's Gran Moravia, a Ukrainian grana padano that's like Parmigiano-Reggiano but less expensive. All our pies use the three-cheese blend and a lot have a parmesan garnish, so they're really four-cheese pies. Oh, and for vegan cheese, we use Follow Your Heart Parmesan and mozzarella. If you want a really big cheese "fence" around

your pies, add a couple more ounces and make sure it's pushed all the way to the edge of the pan.

CHICKEN

We usually roast boneless chicken thighs in house. For a vegan option, Morningstar Farms makes decent frozen vegan chik'n strips with no breading. You can use them the same way.

CURRY PASTE

Maesri makes a red curry paste in a 4-ounce can you can mix with coconut milk. It'll never be as good as pounded fresh spices, but this paste tastes on point and saves a ton of time.

FLOUR

At the shop, we use 50-pound bags of Sir Lancelot high-gluten flour. The King Arthur bread flours you can find everywhere are similar, and it's what we used to test all the recipes in this book.

DRIED FRIED SHALLOTS

Keep a package of these on hand and you'll always have a slammin' last-minute topping for fries, steaks—you name it. They're the finishing touch on our Norf Fries (page 176). Asian grocers carry them and you can find them in well-stocked grocery stores and specialty stores.

JERK SEASONING

We used to use Walkerwood wet jerk seasoning, which is baller, but it's hard to come by. Now, we just use a couple tablespoons of dried jerk seasoning per pound of meat. That's how we make our jerk lamb sausage for Break You Off (page 104) and the jerk turkey sausage for Say Yes (page 110).

MAYONNAISE

Terrafin Creek is the foodservice brand we use, but Duke's or Hellmann's both work fine. For vegan mayo, Follow Your Heart Vegenaise is our go-to.

MONTREAL STEAK SEASONING

This mix flavors our Sautéed Mushrooms (page 55) and Roasted Chicken Thighs (pag 56). It was originally the seasoning on Montreal smoked meat, a kind of pastrami made in Canada, but these days most folks shake it on grilled steaks. McCormick makes a popular version. Other brands make it, too. Or make it yourself: mix 2 tablespoons kosher salt, 2 tablespoons cracked black peppercorns, 1 tablespoon dried minced garlic, 1 tablespoon dried minced onion, 1 tablespoon red pepper flakes, 2 teaspoons mustard seeds, 2 teaspoons dill seeds, 2 teaspoons dried coriander, and 2 teaspoons paprika.

OIL

We used to use two different kinds of oil for sautéing and frying, then prices went up. Now we just use canola.

PIZZA SAUCE

We use Full-Red Pizza Sauce with Basil, in commercial #10 cans, which is about 6 pounds or 11 cups. If you buy that much and don't need it all, you can freeze the extra. You could also use your favorite pizza sauce.

PEPPERONI

We're a halal pizza shop and so we use halal beef pepperoni and turkey pepperoni from Miramar. If you're going vegan, the best plant-based pepperoni we've found is from Field Roast. It dries out a little in the oven, so drizzle on some olive oil when the pizza comes out.

SALT

Diamond Crystal kosher salt is the pro kitchen standby. If we can't get it, we buy another kosher salt. We measure by weight, but if you use spoons, here are some options to replace 2 tablespoons Diamond Crystal kosher salt (16.8 grams): use 1 tablespoon + ½ teaspoon Morton kosher salt, or use 2¾ teaspoons table salt or fine sea salt.

EQUIPMENT

SAUSAGE

At the shop, we mix up our own quick version of halal beef sausage. We also use halal turkey sausage for I'm a Boss (page 106). For vegan sausage, Field Roast makes a decent Italian-style sausage with fennel and garlic. Just crumble it with a fork.

SEAFOOD FRY MIX

For the fried shrimp on our Glamorous Life pizza (page 128), we use a ready-made seasoned breading mix from McCormick called Golden Dipt Seafood Fry Mix.

THAI CHILI SAUCE

Ever had bang bang shrimp? Thai sweet chili sauce is the key. We like Mae Ploy brand on our Thai Chili Wings (page 173).

YEAST

We call for dry yeast in our Down North Pizza Crust (page 30). Both active dry yeast and instant yeast work. The instant gets going a little faster, but the active catches up in the end. We use SAF brand instant yeast because it's cheap and it keeps at room temp for months; it's pretty much the pizza and bread baker's standard yeast. If you buy the big bag rather than the smaller single-use packets, store it in the fridge to keep the yeast active.

BAKING STONES/STEELS

When using a home oven, you'll get a crispier pizza crust with a baking stone or, better yet, a baking steel—and the thicker the better. Go for at least a ½-inch-thick stone or a ¼-inch-thick steel. You need only about a 12-inch square or 12-inch round one to hold one square 10-inch pizza pan. If you plan on baking more than one square pie at a time, get bigger stones or steels.

OVEN

A pizza oven preheated to 700°F works best for our pizzas. At the shop, we use a classic shallow-deck oven. We also tested the recipes in various electric, gas, and wood-fired pizza ovens, and they all turned out square pies with a crunchy browned crust, a fluffy interior, and crispy fried cheese around the edges. A regular home oven works fine; just set the oven to maximum heat (usually 500° or 550°F), with the convection feature turned on if you have it, and place the baking stone or baking steel on a top rack set 6 to 8 inches below the heating element. A baking steel works better than a stone because it transfers more heat to the bottom of your pizza. Either way, preheat the oven for 1 hour with the stone or steel in place so it gets fully heated. That bottom heat is what helps crisp up the crust and create the cheese "fence." Place the pizza on the stone or steel, and bake for 10 minutes or so; if the toppings aren't cooked through or the edges aren't looking browned enough, switch on the oven's broiler for more top heat.

For electric ovens, you may have to open the oven door for 10 seconds to make sure the broiler turns on. Then, with the broiler on, keep baking the pizza for a few more minutes until the edges are nice and browned but not burnt. Watch it like a hawk so it doesn't burn! Your goal is a crisp crust with a dark brown cheese "fence" all around it and some browned cheese on top. If you have raw meat on top, that needs to cook through, too. Just know that all ovens are a little different and most have hot and cool spots. You might have to play around with the temp, timing, and placement of your oven racks to hit the sweet spot.

PIZZA PANS

Lloyd's 10-inch square blue steel pans are the bomb. Their aluminum version is good too. You could get away with heavy 9-inch square cake pans, but the crust will come out a little thicker. We tested our recipes with both Lloyd's pans and heavy-duty 9-inch square aluminum pans from USA Pan. Both worked great.

SCALE

Chefs weigh everything because volume measures like cups and tablespoons can't be trusted. That's because volumes change but weights are constant. Pick up a digital scale that measures in grams. They're cheap. That way you'll get your pizza dough right every time.

SPATULA

A wide metal spatula helps to loosen the pizza and cheese "fence" from the sides of your pizza pan. A 5- or 6-inch wide spatula works best.

SQUIRT BOTTLES

Our pizzas have a signature look with the sauce on top. For thicker sauces like Norf Sauce (page 34) and Wiz Sauce (page 48), we use spoons and ladles to add it over the toppings in big wide stripes. But thinner sauces like Honey Chipotle Sauce (page 43) look better squirted on top in a zigzag pattern. That gives you more even distribution, too. Pick up a standard 16-ounce squirt bottle or smaller 8-ounce or 4-ounce bottles, depending on how many pizzas you'll be making in a single session. (Or reuse something like an empty squirt bottle of sriracha sauce.)

DOUGHS, SAUCES + SUCH

The preps in this chapter are staples in our kitchen. They're our foundation. Our building blocks. I like to cross-utilize, so the Sautéed Mushrooms (page 55) show up on a few pizzas, including P.S.K. (page 68), Uptown Vibes (page 66), and Honcho's Birthday Pie (page 82). The Honey Chipotle Sauce (page 43) is our most popular wing sauce, and we also drizzle it on What We Do (page 96), our meat lover's pizza.

No matter what prep you're making, try to get it done before you start building your pizza. Making pizza is like cooking a stir-fry: You want everything prepped and ready to go before you rock it out. Get the dough made. Sauces mixed. Cheeses shredded. Toppings prepped. Then when it comes time to cook, you can just assemble, bake, cut, and garnish. If you really want to get ahead, you can even parbake the Down North Pizza Crust (page 30) and freeze it for months so it's ready to go whenever you want a pizza. Norf Sauce (page 34) can also be frozen for months. Our wing sauces can chill for days in the fridge. You could even make whole pizzas ahead if you want and stash them in the freezer. Like all pizza, a Down North pizza tastes great reheated the next day—or even cold from the fridge.

—MIKE CARTER

PROPS TO THE DOWN NORTH CREW

Before we opened Down North, we did weekend popups to see if this pizza shop was gonna fly. That's when **Miss Tremelle** came on board. She was from Uplift, a returning citizen re-entry program that helps formerly incarcerated folks get back on their feet and find decent jobs. We taught Miss Tremelle how to bag up our three-cheese mix, run the register, and use chef talk—like saying "behind" when a busy chef couldn't see her walking behind them in the kitchen.

Miss Tremelle's a recovering alcoholic. She and her sister inherited a little money from their family, as well as their father's liquor license. They opened a bar in North Philly called MySpace Lounge, but Miss Tremelle and her brother-in-law didn't see eye-to-eye. So, he'd give Miss Tremelle money to go drink somewhere else. She ended up on the streets, sippin' on handles of cheap Jacquin's vodka.

That's what led to her incarceration. One time, she gave another woman some money to come back with booze, but the woman never came back. They saw each other a few times after that and, according to Miss Tremelle, one time "I said something, and the woman got nasty. . . . I was still giving her some of my liquor at the time, but not as much. And that time, I gave her what she deserved."

That fight got Miss Tremelle five years' jail time for aggravated assault. When she got out, she got clean

Pizza has this ability to bring people together. It's feel-good food that people from all walks of life can get behind. —Muhammad Abdul-Hadi

and came to Down North. She told us how she had always wanted to be a prep cook, and how she loves her grandkids and likes to make banana bread. Our reply? "When do you want to start?" Ever since, Miss Tremelle has been the matriarch of the shop. She softens the male energy of the cooks and she has become the glue that holds things together.

"I feel a part of something here," she says. "There's genuine love at Down North, genuine concern. We're like a family. The guys call me. Ask if I'm okay. I never felt like that in all my years. . . . Chef Mike even asked me to a family cookout over in Lansdowne. For these guys, coming from the streets, doing time, then coming back here to change people's lives, I'm truly grateful. This place keeps me in a peaceful state of mind."

We're grateful, too. Helping people like Miss Tremelle is the whole reason Down North exists.

The same goes for **Myles**, one of our line cooks. In the kitchen, Myles's nickname is 210 Tiny, a joke because he's a big guy. Mike and Myles worked together at Booker's Restaurant & Bar, in West Philly, and when we were building Down North, Myles was still in the county jail for selling drugs. He happened to get released right when we opened, and Mike needed chefs who could actually cook. Myles fit the employment criteria and was a total kitchen pro, working the line faster than anyone else I've ever seen. He's the guy who suggested using lamb sausage to make Break You Off (page 104), one of our signature pizzas.

Perm is another guy who turned his life around at Down North. Perm did fifteen years: six for armed robbery, five for drug possession, and four for possession of a firearm. After he was released from federal prison, Perm came to the shop and found something he'd never seen before: good role models. He was now in a positive environment with people who showed him a better path forward in life. "I don't like to be around bad energy," says Perm. "The brotherhood at Down North is cool. Everybody's on the same vibe." He learned everything, from how to cook chicken wings and pizzas to how to make guests feel welcome. At first, Perm wasn't too culinarily inclined, but he was good at following directions and he figured out how to work as part of a team—important skills for any job.

At this point, dozens of formerly incarcerated men and women like Miss Tremelle, Myles, and Perm have come through the shop. They've redirected their lives away from the streets and found good-paying jobs. That's what we do at Down North, and pizza is the vehicle that gets it done. Pizza has this ability to bring people together. It's feel-good food that people from all walks of life can get behind. Some remember those cheesy square slices from Friday afternoons at the school cafeteria. Others remember the square pizza straight from the toaster oven. Some remember it from parties in the neighborhood. And others remember pizza as one of the only halfway decent things served in prison. But for everyone, it's a source of comfort. A source of joy.

DOWN NORTH PIZZA CRUST

Here's three great things about this dough: (1) You don't have to knead it. (2) It's ready in under 2 hours. (3) You can make it ahead and freeze it for later (both before baking and after). That means you can satisfy a pizza craving with scratch-made dough in very little time. At the shop, we use this parbake method to speed up production. In a happy accident, we also found out that parbaking makes the dough shrink back from the pan, which allows us to create a bigger crust of cheese (that cheese "fence") around the edges. Another plus: parbaking means your crust will be ready whenever you are—whether that's now or next month (if you're freezing for later). When you make this dough, if at all possible, weigh your ingredients because weights are much more accurate than volume measures.

2⅛ cups (500 g) lukewarm water

1 tablespoon + ½ teaspoon (12 g) dry yeast, active or instant

2⅓ teaspoons (10 g) sugar

4⅔ cups (635 g) unbleached bread flour, such as King Arthur

2¼ tablespoons (30 g) extra-virgin olive oil, plus 4 tablespoons (53 g) for greasing and shaping

2⅔ tablespoons (22 g) kosher salt

Make the dough: Put the water, yeast, and sugar in the bowl of an electric mixer. Whisk briefly, then set aside until the yeast looks foamy, 5 to 10 minutes.

Add the flour and the 2¼ tablespoons olive oil, then attach the dough hook. Set the mixer to speed 2 (about medium-low) and let it rock until the dough is mixed and looks kinda ropy and sticky, 10 to 12 minutes. Scrape down the sides of the bowl, if necessary, then add the salt and set the mixer to speed 3. Let it rock again until the dough is firm and smoother but still sticky; that'll take another 10 minutes or so. (Don't worry about the dough coming together into a ball; this dough is so loose it won't do that.)

At this point, you can freeze the raw dough in a 1½- to 2-quart covered container for up to a month. Thaw the dough in the refrigerator overnight before using the next day.

Prepare the pans: Generously oil two 10-inch square baking pans (see page 23) with about 2 tablespoons oil each. Get the bottoms and sides greased up good. (If you have only one pan, oil it and proof half the dough in it. Keep the other half of dough covered in the refrigerator until you're ready to bake it. After the first dough is parbaked and cooling on the rack, let the

1600 The transatlantic slave trade is established, a brutal apparatus of European colonialism sustained by European imperialism to institutionalize coerced human labor.[2]

pan cool for a few minutes, then repeat the process of oiling the same pan and proofing and parbaking the second dough in it.)

Preheat the oven: If you have a pizza oven, preheat it to 700°F. In a home oven, set the temperature for maximum heat (500° or 550°F), with the convection setting on if you have it, and put a baking stone or baking steel (see page 23) on a top rack of the oven set 6 to 8 inches below the heat. Preheat the oven for 1 hour.

Proof the dough: Cut the dough into two equal halves and add one half to each pan. Dip your fingers in water, then press the dough out a little in the pan. The dough won't fill the pans just yet, but press it out as far as you can. Wrap the pans in plastic (a plastic shopping bag works great, too) and let the dough proof at room temperature until it expands to cover most of each pan, 20 to 30 minutes. If your room is hot, the proofing might take only 10 to 15 minutes.

Proof the dough again: Unwrap the pans and coat your dominant hand with a bit of oil. Use your oily hand to press the dough all the way into the corners of each pan in an even layer. If you need to, pull at the dough corners gently to fill the pans. Wrap the pans again and let the dough proof again until each has risen and puffed up, kinda like Mike Tyson's face after a bout in the ring—20 to 30 minutes in a comfy room or 10 to 15 minutes in a hot room.

Parbake the dough: When the oven is to temperature, set the pans on the stone or steel and parbake the dough until the crusts pull away from the edges of the pans, the tops look dry but not too browned, and the bottoms look golden (use a wide metal spatula to check the undersides), 3 to 4 minutes at 700°F or 5 to 7 minutes at 500°F. If the bottoms aren't golden, pop the pans back in the oven for another minute or two.

Cool the dough: Remove the pans from the oven and set them on a wire rack to cool for a bit—at least 15 minutes or up to 4 hours. After an hour of cooling, cover the pans so the dough doesn't dry out.

Finish or save: At this point, you can top and finish baking the pizzas immediately. Or save the parbaked crusts for later; transfer the cooled crusts from the pans to freezer-weight zippered plastic bags or other containers. Seal and refrigerate for 10 to 15 days (or freeze up to 15 months). Thaw overnight in the fridge before using. To finish the pizzas, place the thawed crusts back into the pans and follow the instructions in the pizza recipes for topping and baking. For an extra-crunchy crust, generously re-oil the sides and bottom of the pans before adding the parbaked crusts.

remix

COCO BREAD CRUST: For our collab pizza with Aunts et Uncles in Brooklyn (see page 161), I give our crust the taste of Jamaican coco bread by stirring 1 teaspoon coconut extract into the water and yeast mixture along with the flour and oil.

MIND THE HUMIDITY

When I was working on the dough before we opened Down North, I wanted the crust to be fluffy inside but nice and crisp outside, so I took the hydration (amount of water added) up real high. Then Philly's summer humidity threw me a curveball, and with the high humidity and all the water I added to the mix, the dough got so loose it was slipping like slime! But the crust came out so good. It seemed like the more water we added, the better the crust got, so Mar (see page 91) and I kept playing. Now we got the hydration and everything else with this dough dialed. It makes *the best* Philly-style pan pizza.

The first few times you make our pizza dough, measure the water on a scale to keep that variable constant. That way, if you notice differences between batches of dough (one is looser, or stickier, etc.), you'll know it's due to humidity and not the amount of water you added. Then you can adjust the water the next time you mix the dough. Every kitchen is different, and humidity in the air varies with the time of year. If the air is dry, your dough may need more water added, and if it's humid, it may need less water.

JULY 1640 The first instance of racial disparity in legal retribution: Three runaway indentured servants are captured in Virginia. As punishment, two white servants are given additional years of servitude, while the Black man is enslaved for life.[3]

**MAKES ABOUT
1 QUART (4 CUPS),
ENOUGH FOR
ABOUT 4 PIZZAS**

In 2013, I came home from prison after spending twelve years upstate. One of my good friends is a New York Giants football fan, while I'm a Dallas Cowboys fan. (I know what you're thinking: a Cowboys fan in Philly . . . howzat? What can I say?) Anyway, we bet on the NFL season opener that fall, and I won the bet so she had to take me out to dinner. She took me to one of them Italian mom-and-pop joints in Jersey. And that's where I got an education in arrabbiata sauce. I've been making spicy red sauce forever—I just didn't know it was called arrabbiata in Italian, which literally translates to "angry." I love spicy food, and whenever I eat pizza, I always shake some red pepper flakes onto it. When it was time to make a signature Down North (or Norf, as we call it) pizza sauce, I knew it was going to pack some heat. Gimme the angry sauce. I added some dried oregano, onion, garlic, and liquid smoke, which *sends* it. I go through five gallons of it a day.

---

1 (28-ounce) can pizza sauce (see page 22; about 3½ cups)

1 cup warm water

½ cup sugar

⅓ cup red pepper flakes

⅔ cup dried oregano

5 tablespoons onion powder

5 tablespoons garlic powder

1 teaspoon liquid smoke

With a stick blender or in a stand blender, combine the pizza sauce, water, sugar, red pepper flakes, oregano, onion powder, garlic powder, and liquid smoke. The mixture should be kinda thick, not runny, and still spoonable. (You can adjust the thickness by adding more water, if you need to.)

Pour the sauce into a covered container and store at room temp if you're using it within a day, or refrigerate it for up to a week or freeze it for up to 2 months.

remix

NOT VODKA SAUCE: Add 1 cup heavy cream, 4 tablespoons (½ stick) melted unsalted butter, ½ cup grated parmesan, and 1 tablespoon Old Bay seasoning along with the water. Blend until smooth.

1662–1676 Black bodies are legally codified as Virginia's 1662 law establishes hereditary slavery through Black women, ushering in the transition from indentured servitude to Black slavery.[4]

1703 Boston passes a curfew law for Black and Indigenous people, criminalizing the movements of Black and Indigenous bodies.[5]

NORFFALO SAUCE

My goal here was to make a bomb-ass buffalo sauce. I fucked with the Frank's RedHot and the Sweet Baby Ray's Nashville Hot and the butter—a key ingredient in legit buffalo sauce. It all came together and the recipe hasn't changed since. This sauce is just spicy enough and goes on our Yeah That's Us Pizza (page 100), Norffalo Wings (page 170), and Vegan Norffalo Cauliflower Wings (page 174). It starts with a *beurre monté* (fancy French name for melted butter that stays smooth and creamy) so the sauce can be kept emulsified in a squirt bottle at room temp. Perfect for zigzagging over anything that needs a little oomph, from french fries to scrambled eggs.

¼ cup (½ stick) cold unsalted butter, cut into chunks

1 cup Frank's RedHot sauce

1 cup Sweet Baby Ray's Nashville Hot Wing Sauce

We gonna turn the butter into *beurre monté* so it stays emulsified (smooth) in the sauce. It's simple: Place a couple tablespoons of water in a medium saucepan over high heat. When it comes to a boil, cut the heat to low, tilt the pan, and whisk in a chunk or two of butter in the corner of the pan. When that melts, whisk in a couple more chunks. Keep whisking in the rest of the butter.

Then whisk in the Frank's and Sweet Baby Ray's sauces. Keep the sauce warm over low heat in the saucepan until ready to use or store.

For squirting, pour the sauce into a squirt bottle and put the bottle in a saucepan of warm water to keep it warm. Or, chill the sauce for later in the bottle or in a lidded container for up to 2 weeks. Rewarm in the microwave or in a warm water bath before using.

remix
VEGAN NORFFALO SAUCE: Use vegan butter. It works just as well.

1705 The Virginia Slave Codes legally enshrine slavery as a racial capitalist institution, including slave patrols and the apprehension of runaway slaves, laying the foundation for modern policing.[6]

FEBRUARY 1793 Congress passes the Fugitive Slave Act and later the Fugitive Slave Act of 1850, formally establishing slave patrols as the law of the land.[7]

HOUSE BBQ SAUCE

When we opened Down North, I had no life. I was literally waking up, walking my dog, going to the kitchen for sixteen hours, walking my dog again, then going to sleep. Making our BBQ sauce from scratch was getting to be too much. This simpler sauce still slaps (gochujang, or Korean red chili paste, really knocks the flavor up) and it's so much easier. For the more complex recipe, check out the Flip Side BBQ Sauce (page 39).

1 cup Bull's Eye Original BBQ Sauce

1 cup KC Masterpiece Mesquite BBQ Sauce

¼ cup gochujang (Korean red chili paste)

Add the BBQ sauces and gochujang to a medium bowl and whisk until smooth. If it's too thick, whisk in a little water, 1 tablespoon at a time. The sauce should be medium-thick and squirtable, like your typical Kansas City BBQ sauce.

the game

If we run out of gochujang, we use 3 tablespoons gochugaru (Korean red chili flakes) instead. Grind the flakes in a spice grinder or clean coffee mill until it's a coarse powder, then stir it into the BBQ sauces.

1856 Bridget Mason, a Black slave, successfully sues for her and her family's freedom in California, a free state.[8]

MARCH 6, 1857 The U.S. Supreme Court rules in *Dred Scott v. Sandford* that Black people are not U.S. citizens, effectively denying any Black person, enslaved or free, from petitioning the federal government about their grievances, including their right to liberty and freedom from tyranny and oppression.[9]

JANUARY 1, 1863 President Abraham Lincoln signs the Emancipation Proclamation into law, decreeing the end of slavery in the United States with a Union Army victory in the Civil War.

FLIP SIDE BBQ SAUCE

I like black pepper beef jerky. Black pepper Cooper Cheese. Black pepper *everything.* Thanks to my mom and the Oregon Asian market in South Philly, I discovered Lee Kum Kee's black pepper sauce. That's my secret weapon here. You can get it at most Asian markets or online. I started marinating meats with it, and then eventually began incorporating it into my super-secret family BBQ sauce recipe. Here's my version of that recipe. (Yeah, you're not getting the super-secret one.)

1 sweet onion (like Vidalia or Maui)

1 tablespoon vegetable oil

1 (28-ounce) can tomato sauce

½ cup Lee Kum Kee Black Pepper Sauce

½ cup apple cider vinegar

⅓ cup honey

¼ cup tomato paste

¼ cup molasses

3 tablespoons Worcestershire sauce

2 teaspoons liquid smoke

2 teaspoons dry mustard powder

1 teaspoon smoked paprika

1 teaspoon garlic powder

½ teaspoon onion powder

½ teaspoon kosher salt

½ teaspoon freshly ground black pepper

About ½-inch piece fresh ginger, peeled

½ to 1 teaspoon cayenne (if you like it hot)

Cut two ⅛-inch-thick slices from the center of the onion so you have two thick discs. Pull off and discard the peels from those discs. Add the oil to a medium saucepan over medium-low heat, then add the onion slices, breaking them up into rings, and cook low and slow until they are caramelized and dark brown, about 30 minutes, stirring now and then for even browning. (If you need to speed things up, raise the heat a bit and every time the onion slices are getting dark brown, swirl a little water in the pan to deglaze, then use a wooden spoon to mix the browned goodness into the onion pieces. That cuts the cooking time almost in half.)

Add the tomato sauce, black pepper sauce, vinegar, honey, tomato paste, molasses, Worcestershire sauce, liquid smoke, dry mustard, smoked paprika, garlic powder, onion powder, salt, pepper, ginger, and cayenne (if using). Whisk together and bring to a simmer over medium-high heat. Then drop the heat to medium-low and simmer until the sauce thickens a bit, 20 to 30 minutes, stirring now and then.

Use a stick blender in the saucepan or transfer to a stand blender and process until the sauce is nice and smooth. (If you want to be sure, pour it through a sieve to strain out any stray chunks of onion or ginger.) Use immediately (we keep it in squirt bottles) or refrigerate for up to a week or freeze for a couple of months.

QUICK THAI RED CURRY SAUCE

I made this Thai red curry jawn for Sauce It Up (page 124), the spicy pizza I served on the First We Feast's show *Pizza Wars.* A can of Maesri's red curry paste brings the heat and spice. Fresh ginger, fresh lime zest, and a little fish sauce contribute the rest. You need only about ½ cup sauce for a pizza. Toss the leftover sauce with cooked noodles for a Thai noodle bowl. Or simmer some mussels in the sauce. To keep this sauce vegan, use vegan fish sauce.

1 (14-ounce) can full-fat coconut milk

1 (4-ounce) can red curry paste, such as Maesri

Finely grated zest of 1 Makrut lime (see The Game)

2 tablespoons fish sauce

1 (1½-inch) piece fresh ginger, peeled and finely chopped (about 1 tablespoon)

Combine the coconut milk, curry paste, lime zest, fish sauce, and ginger in a medium saucepan. Bring to a simmer over medium-high heat, then reduce the heat to medium-low and simmer gently until the flavors blend and the sauce thickens a bit, 15 to 20 minutes.

Puree the sauce until smooth using a stick blender in the saucepan or using a stand blender. Let cool a few minutes, then use immediately or refrigerate in an airtight container for up to a week.

the game

Look for fresh Makrut limes in Asian markets. They have bumpy, dark green peels with tons of floral aroma. If you can't find a Makrut, use a standard Persian lime.

JUNE 19, 1865 Black people enslaved in the Confederate state of Texas finally learn about their freedom from an executive decree when Union Army soldiers arrive in Galveston Bay, Texas, to make the announcement. This date is thereafter remembered as Juneteenth.[10]

DECEMBER 6, 1865 The 13th Amendment to the Constitution outlaws slavery in the United States with one key exception: the allowance of slavery as a form of punishment for people convicted of crimes. This exception lays the foundation for penal labor and convict leasing, a form of indentured servitude whereby incarcerated Black people are sent to fill labor shortages after the Civil War.[11,12]

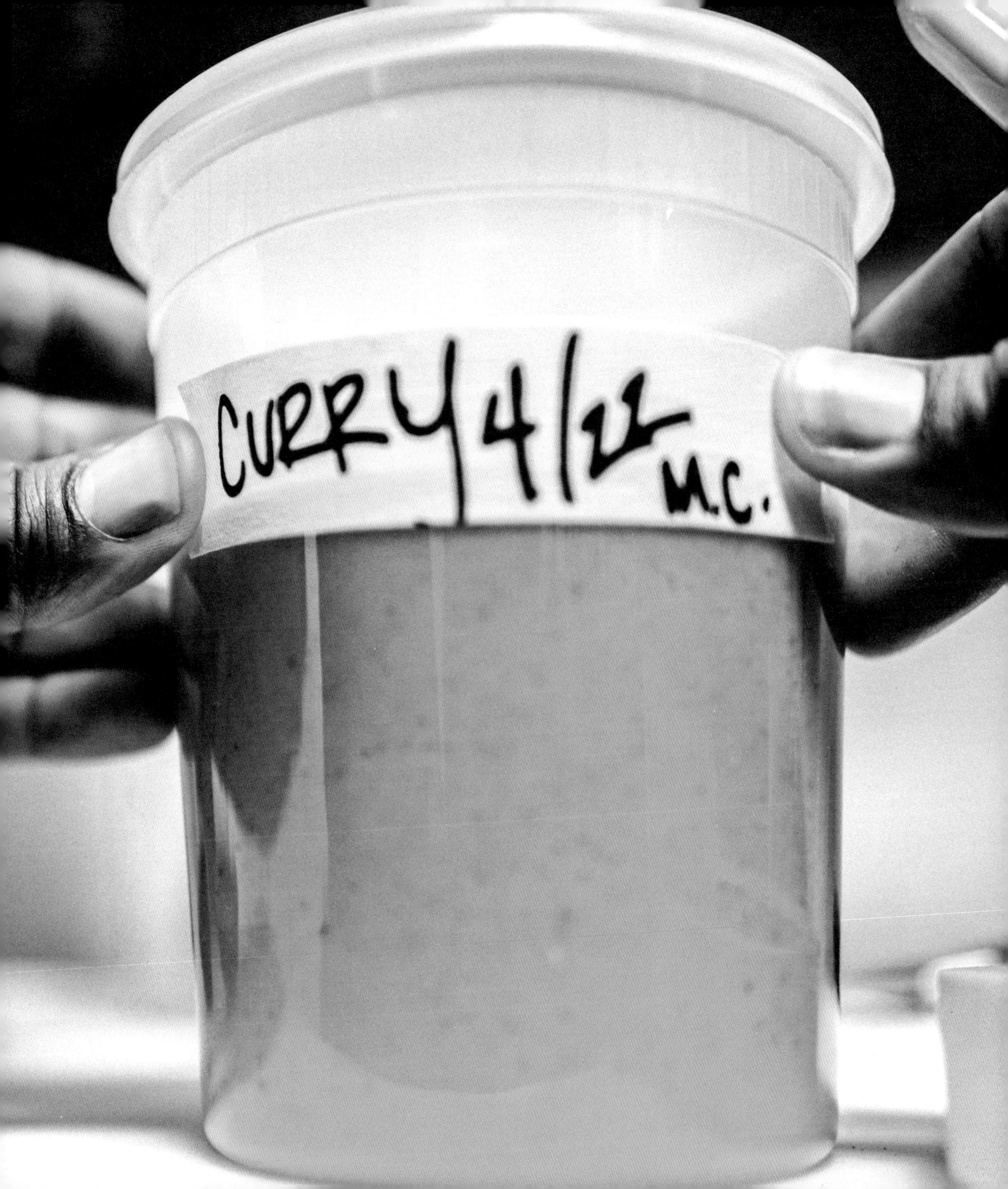
CURRY 4/22
M.C.

MAKES A LITTLE
OVER 2 CUPS

HONEY CHIPOTLE SAUCE

This was one of the first sauces we had on the menu. We drizzled it over our meat lover's pizza, What We Do (page 96). Now, I put this swicy sauce on our wings. The Honey Chipotle Wings (page 173) became a top seller for people who don't like their wings too spicy; and the smoke from the chipotle and the sweet from the honey work magic here.

1 cup mayonnaise

⅔ cup honey

2 tablespoons chipotle powder

½ cup water

Add the mayonnaise, honey, chipotle powder, and water to a medium bowl and whisk to combine. Keep chilled until ready to use (mayonnaise goes bad after a few hours out of refrigeration).

remix

ROASTED GARLIC–HONEY CHIPOTLE SAUCE: Instead of using plain honey, try our roasted garlic honey (see Break You Off pizza, step 1, page 105). Bumps up the flavor even more.

JANUARY 12, 1865 Black people are promised 40 acres and a mule to live independently, but this attempt at reparations never comes to fruition, with the assassination of President Abraham Lincoln and his successor, Andrew Johnson, overturning Special Field Order No. 15.[13]

1865–1866 Black codes emerge as a system of laws that replicate slavery and the social control of Black people in a racist backlash to emancipation.[14]

BASIL PESTO

I think I first started making a version of this pesto at Vedge, Philly's top vegan restaurant. But it could have been earlier. And I've changed it over the years. Either way, this is the version I use most often now. If you've never made pesto yourself, know that it's dead easy—and better than anything you'll get off the shelf. Go for real Parmigiano-Reggiano cheese for the best flavor.

2 cups packed fresh basil leaves (about 2 ounces)

⅔ cup grated parmesan cheese

¼ cup grated pecorino cheese

¼ cup pine nuts (not toasted)

¼ cup extra-virgin olive oil

2 medium garlic cloves

½ teaspoon sea salt, or more as needed

Pinch of freshly ground black pepper, or more as needed

Add the basil, parmesan, pecorino, pine nuts, olive oil, garlic, salt, and pepper to a food processor or mini chopper and blend until mostly smooth. Taste and add more salt and pepper if you think it needs it. Refrigerate any leftovers for up to a week or freeze in an airtight container for a couple of months.

remix
BASIL-PESTO CREAM SAUCE: Blend about ½ cup heavy cream and ¼ cup melted unsalted butter into the pesto.

the game
If you need a shortcut, Cento sells jars of organic basil pesto imported from Italy. They ain't bad. The chilled tubs of pesto from Buitoni are passable, too.

MARCH 3, 1865 Congress establishes the Freedmen's Bureau to support, provide relief, and help Black people with basic needs and to manage land abandoned or seized during the Civil War. The majority of the bureau's work concludes in 1868.[15]

44

MAKES ABOUT
3 CUPS

SPICY CHEESE SAUCE

Our fully loaded Norf Fries (page 176) get ladled with this creamy cheese sauce, and they're the best fries ever. The sauce is creamy, savory, and just-enough spicy. You can also toss it with pasta or rice, or drizzle it over roasted veggie or tortilla chips for nachos, or use it anywhere else you want a light cheese sauce with a little heat.

2 cups heavy cream

1½ cups grated parmesan cheese

½ cup sriracha sauce

Pour the cream into a medium saucepan and bring to a simmer over medium-high heat (watch so that the cream doesn't boil over when it comes to a simmer). Remove the saucepan from the heat and whisk in the parmesan and the sriracha. Use right away or refrigerate in a covered container for up to 4 days. Re-warm gently on the stovetop or in a microwave before using.

1865–1876 Reconstruction is a period of racial violence and terror meted out against Black people as they seek to integrate into broader society as equals. This additional wave of racist backlash occurs in response to the rapid political, economic, and social achievements of Black people. Lynching mobs and the Ku Klux Klan become defining engineers of the harsh, violent repudiation of Black progress and integration.[16]

1866–1940s Sharecropping emerges as an exploitative system of tenant farming that mimics de facto enslavement of Black people, retying them to the land through discrimination, terrorism, and violence, and legally barring Black people from owning land.[17,18]

GARLIC—

Here's a quick take on an alfredo sauce, with two forms of onion and two forms of garlic . . . a quad shot of onion and garlic! With all that flavor and the savory parmesan, too, it doesn't need any salt. This is the bomb on chicken wings (see page 173) and our seafood pizza, Glamorous Life (page 128).

Canola oil, for frying

½ yellow onion, roughly chopped (about ½ cup)

½ cup (1 stick) unsalted butter

½ cup heavy cream

¼ cup grated parmesan cheese

2 tablespoons mashed Roasted Garlic Confit (see sidebar, page 47)

1½ teaspoons garlic powder

1½ teaspoons onion powder

½ teaspoon freshly ground black pepper

1 teaspoon ground white pepper

Heat a thin film of the oil in a medium saucepan over medium heat, then add the chopped onion. Rock it out until the onion caramelizes to a deep golden brown, 10 to 15 minutes, stirring now and then to keep it from burning. (If you see a brown film forming on the bottom of the pan, stir in a little water, about 2 tablespoons, to deglaze the pan.)

Add the butter and cream. When the butter has melted, bring the mixture to a simmer over medium-high heat, whisking until fairly smooth. Remove from the heat and whisk in the parmesan, garlic confit, garlic powder, onion powder, black pepper, and white pepper. Whisk like nobody's business until the cheese melts and the sauce is nice and creamy. It should take only a minute, and the consistency should be kinda thick, like the cheese sauce you'd spoon over a cheesesteak.

Use a stick blender right in the pot or transfer to a stand blender to process until the sauce is nice and smooth. If you're not using the sauce right away, keep it warm over the lowest possible heat or add it to a squeeze bottle and keep warm in a pot of warm water.

1871 The Virginia Supreme Court declares that an incarcerated person is a "slave of the state."[19]

PARM SAUCE

ROASTED GARLIC CONFIT

Garlic confit is like rich, roasted garlic, and you can use it wherever you'd use roasted garlic. Whisk it into Norf Sauce (page 34), Norffalo Sauce (page 35), House BBQ Sauce (page 38), Spicy Cheese Sauce (page 45), or Wiz Sauce (page 48)—or just mix it into mashed potatoes.

We started making this confit because we buy peeled garlic cloves in bulk for the shop, which is cheaper and faster than breaking down whole heads of garlic. While most roasted garlic recipes instruct you to roast the whole heads in the skins, when you roast just the peeled cloves in oil, you get this confit instead. You not only get the creamy roasted garlic cloves but also the garlic-infused oil to use for other dishes.

To roast the garlic in oil, preheat the oven to 350°F. Put 2 garlic heads' worth of peeled cloves (about 20 cloves; buy a container of peeled garlic to save time) in a large oven-safe ramekin or baking dish (about 6-ounce capacity). Pour in enough olive oil to barely cover the cloves. (You can add kosher salt, pepper, and herbs, but I usually leave it plain so the garlic and garlic oil are more versatile.)

Place the ramekin on a small sheet pan and bake, uncovered, until the cloves are golden and tender, 45 minutes to 1 hour. Remove from the oven and set aside to cool in the ramekin. Then cover and chill. The roasted cloves will keep for weeks. The oil will solidify when cold, but liquefy again if left out at room temp (or nuke it for 15 seconds). Simply use a fork to lift the cloves out of the oil when you need them, and you're good to go.

For mashed roasted garlic confit, just mash a few cloves with a fork. You'll get 1 to 2 tablespoons mashed garlic from about 10 cloves. To make more, just double or triple the garlic amounts here and add more oil as needed to cover.

1877—1950 A period of sustained lynching in twenty out of fifty states, continuing the violent enforcement of racial hierarchy.[20]

You want homemade Cheez Whiz? Here it is—dead simple. This sauce gets drizzled over our cheesesteak pizza, My Part of Town (page 114). The spicy harissa version goes on Tales of a Hustler (page 117). I add onion and garlic powders to bump up the flavor, but let's be real. You're here for the pure hit of fatty, melty cheese.

If you have any of this sauce left over, spoon it liberally over vegetables, nachos, or tacos; serve it as a warm queso dip; or toss it with cooked elbows for mac 'n cheese.

½ cup heavy cream

1 cup shredded sharp yellow cheddar cheese

¼ teaspoon garlic powder

¼ teaspoon onion powder

Kosher salt, if needed

Pour the cream into a medium saucepan and bring to a simmer over high heat (don't let it boil over). Cut the heat to low and add the cheese, garlic powder, and onion powder. Whisk like nobody's business until the cheese melts and the sauce is nice and creamy. It should only take a minute or two, and the consistency should be kinda thick, like the cheese sauce you'd spoon over a cheesesteak. Taste it and give it a little salt if you think it needs it. Personally, I'm not a big salt guy.

If not using the sauce right away, let it cool, cover it, and refrigerate for up to 2 days. Re-whisk and warm it over low heat, stirring occasionally, until the sauce gets good and creamy again.

remix

HARISSA CHEESE SAUCE: Add 3 to 4 teaspoons spicy harissa paste (we use Mina brand) to the cream along with the cheese. After the sauce thickens, pour it into a blender for a smoother consistency and more consistent deep orange color (or use a stick blender right in the pot), but you don't absolutely have to. Either way, this spicy Wiz Sauce is baller on our Tales of a Hustler Pizza (page 117).

BEER CHEESE SAUCE: Add ½ can of lager to the pot along with the cream. When it comes to a simmer, continue to cook until the consistency is like heavy cream, then cut the heat to low and add the cheese, garlic powder, and onion powder.

1885 The mayor of New Orleans directs the police to arrest any Black man that "did not want to work" during the levee workers' strike.[21]

1888 The Supreme Court of California rules in *Wysinger v. Crookshank* that school segregation of Black people in California is against the law.[22]

VEGAN WIZ SAUCE

When I was growing up, my mom would cube and roast rutabagas, then serve them as a side dish. They're kinda bland, but I always liked how they got creamy inside. Later, when I worked at V Street, a vegan spot in Philly, I cooked with rutabagas and eventually turned them into this sauce for Down North. The rutabaga gives the sauce a thick creaminess and an earthy, mild potato flavor, while the nutritional yeast adds that funky tang you're looking for in cheese. With a big hit of Dijon mustard and some gochugaru (Korean red chili flakes), this sauce has got it going on.

We spoon this sauce on our Vegan Everything Fries (page 182) and Vegan Spicy Crab Fries (page 182). You could also toss it with noodles or ladle it over a mushroom cheesesteak.

1 large rutabaga (about 2 pounds)

½ cup nutritional yeast

½ cup Dijon mustard

1 cup vegan mayonnaise

1 teaspoon freshly ground black pepper

2 teaspoons gochugaru (Korean red chili flakes)

Kosher salt

Peel and roughly cube the rutabaga (in about 1½-inch pieces), then drop the pieces into a medium saucepan. Add enough water to cover the pieces by 1 inch, put the lid on, and bring to a boil over high heat. When the water boils, uncover and continue to boil the rutabaga until tender, 10 to 12 minutes.

Transfer the rutabaga and 2 cups of the cooking liquid to a blender. Add the nutritional yeast and blend until smooth, then add the mustard, mayo, pepper, and chili flakes. Blend again briefly, then taste and season with salt until it works for you.

If you're not serving it right away, transfer to a covered container and refrigerate for up to 2 weeks. Reheat the sauce over low heat in a saucepan, then serve.

the game
To really distribute the heat, grind the gochugaru to a powder in a clean spice grinder or coffee mill before using.

1896 The U.S. Supreme Court legitimizes a "separate but equal" doctrine in the seminal post-Reconstruction case, *Plessy v. Ferguson*. This ruling sustains Jim Crow laws begun in the 1870s as a legalized system of racial segregation in the South and paves the way for racial segregation in the North.[23,24]

VEGAN CAESAR DRESSING

This dressing puts the spark in Honcho's Birthday Pie (page 82). Don't skip the nutritional yeast. It adds a savory flavor that stands in for the anchovies in a traditional Caesar dressing. Look for nutritional yeast (a.k.a., nooch) in a health food store or at Whole Foods. The pizza needs only about ¼ cup of the dressing. Save the remaining for your favorite salad—it keeps in the fridge for up to a week.

½ cup vegan mayonnaise

1 tablespoon Dijon mustard

1 tablespoon extra-virgin olive oil

½ tablespoon nutritional yeast

½ tablespoon drained capers

½ medium garlic clove

Juice of 1 lemon

¾ teaspoon sherry vinegar

¾ teaspoon freshly ground black pepper

¼ teaspoon kosher salt

1 to 2 tablespoons water

Add the mayo, mustard, olive oil, nutritional yeast, capers, garlic, lemon juice, sherry vinegar, pepper, and salt to a blender or small food processor. Blend until smooth, then drizzle in the water—just enough to make a medium-thin salad dressing. Use right away or chill in a covered container for a week.

1905 The Pennsylvania State Police is established, the country's first state police department. By the 1930s, every state has its own state police department.[25]

VEGAN THOUSAND ISLAND DRESSING

I was experimenting with a vegan Reuben sandwich made with smoked beets instead of pastrami, and that idea turned into a banger of a vegan pizza, called Sara Smile (page 78). Smoked beets top the pizza, then this dressing ties the whole pie together. Refrigerate any leftover dressing in an airtight container for up to a month. It's a natural on a green salad.

¼ cup sauerkraut

¼ cup ketchup

1 tablespoon drained capers

1 tablespoon roughly chopped red onion

1 tablespoon roughly chopped fresh dill

1 heaping tablespoon roughly chopped chives

1 heaping tablespoon Dijon mustard

1 heaping tablespoon extra-virgin olive oil

1 cup vegan mayonnaise

1 heaping tablespoon sriracha sauce

Put the sauerkraut, ketchup, capers, onion, dill, chives, mustard, and olive oil in a mini-chopper, then pulse until everything is finely chopped. You don't want it totally smooth. (You can also mince the solid ingredients by hand, if you want, then mix in the creamy stuff.) Scrape the mix into a medium bowl and whisk in the mayo and sriracha. Use right away, or chill in a covered container for up to a month.

1915–1960 During the Great Migration, millions of Black people migrate from the South to the North, Midwest, and Western states to pursue economic and educational opportunities, find a better quality of life, and escape racial violence. Rich culinary traditions follow this mass movement, as Black Americans establish food businesses around the country.[26,27]

1919 A series of anti-Black riots known as the Red Summer of 1919 culminates in the lynching and brutal murder of Will Brown, a 40-year-old Black man accused of raping a 19-year-old white woman after the local newspaper sensationalizes the story and 250 men and women form a lynch mob outside the Omaha Courthouse where Brown is being held.[28,29]

PIKLIZ

These are Haitian pickles. Translation: they're hella hot. I first tasted them at my friend's house. Her husband is Haitian, and she made some John-John, the Haitian black mushroom and rice dish with boiled chicken, and she served it with pikliz. She told me, "Pikliz is the heat you add to your meat." Once I tasted it, I knew it would end up on a pizza someday.

First, I saved it for something special: a smoked brisket pizza, one of those things I'd been playing around with for years. After a little trial and error, these spicy pickles, that smoky brisket, and some Harissa Cheese Sauce came together in Tales of a Hustler (page 117). You could also put the pickles in an Italian sandwich instead of giardiniera. Or, serve it as the pickles on your cheese board. Or, just eat them.

1 cup thinly sliced green cabbage

1 small carrot, thinly sliced into julienned strips (about ½ cup)

2 shallots, halved and thinly sliced (about ¼ cup)

2 Scotch bonnet chiles

2 sprigs of fresh thyme, plus some leaves for garnish

2 whole cloves

1 teaspoon kosher salt

3 tablespoons fresh lime juice

Distilled white vinegar, for pickling (a couple of cups)

Pack the cabbage, carrot, shallots, chiles, thyme sprigs, and cloves into a 1-pint glass mason jar. Add the salt and lime juice, then fill the jar with vinegar to cover the ingredients. Screw on the lid and shake until the ingredients are well mixed.

Let the pikliz sit at room temp for at least 1 day or even a few days. Then keep it stored in the fridge for months; it'll get stronger the longer it sits.

MAY 31, 1921 The Tulsa Oklahoma Race Massacre thwarts Black progress and economic mobility in a pivotal example of state-sanctioned racist terrorism.[30] The massacre systematically destroys the prosperous Black community of Greenwood, commonly known as Black Wall Street, as more than 1,000 Black-owned businesses and homes are obliterated.[31,32]

1931—1937 Nine young Black men are falsely accused of raping two white women aboard a train near Scottsboro, Alabama. The men are convicted, with eight sentenced to death and one to life imprisonment. The Scottsboro Boys trial and Defense Campaign ensues, resulting in their freedom, although it is almost twenty years before the last young man is released.[33]

SAUTÉED MUSHROOMS

Mushrooms are like vegan meat, so I season them like meat with Montreal steak seasoning. These mushrooms flavor our signature vegan pizza, P.S.K. (page 68); our veggie pie, Uptown Vibes (page 66); and our turkey lover's pizza, I'm a Boss (page 106). We even put an Old Bay spin on them for our Vegan Spicy Crab Fries (page 182). The amount here makes enough for one pizza or one serving of fries.

About 2 tablespoons olive oil or vegetable oil

4 ounces fresh shiitake mushrooms, tough stems removed and caps thinly sliced (1¼ cups)

4 ounces fresh oyster mushrooms, stems trimmed, remainder cut into bite-sized pieces (small ones left whole) (1¼ cups)

About 1 tablespoon Montreal steak seasoning

Heat the olive oil in a medium skillet over medium heat. Once it's shimmering, add the mushrooms and season liberally with the Montreal seasoning. Cook until some of the water given off by the mushrooms evaporates and they're just starting to brown but are still plump and meaty, 4 to 5 minutes, with some stirring now and then. Remove from the heat and use within an hour or refrigerate in an airtight container for up to 2 days.

remix

OLD BAY MUSHROOMS: Replace the Montreal seasoning with Old Bay seasoning, and instead of sautéing, toss the mushrooms with the seasoning and oil, then spread in a sheet pan and roast in a 375°F oven until some of the mushroom water has evaporated but the mushrooms are still plump and meaty, 4 to 5 minutes, stirring a couple times.

1930 The Civil Rights movement begins.[34]

1930 The Federal Bureau of Investigation (FBI) is established. Under J. Edgar Hoover's leadership, the FBI becomes responsible for COINTELPRO, a federal government project that includes sabotaging legitimate[35] political dissent and the hyper-surveillance of Black people, their lives, and organized resistance to structural racism.[36,37]

ROASTED
CHICKEN
THIGHS

MAKES ABOUT
2½ CUPS CUBED
MEAT

When I first made our buffalo chicken pizza, Yeah That's Us (page 100), I used chicken breasts. But they were drying out too much, so I switched to thighs, which are my favorite part of the bird anyway. Now we also use this prep on our BBQ chicken pizza, Big Head (page 103), and our pesto chicken pizza, A Long Walk (page 122).

Chicken can be boring, but when you use thighs and you season 'em like this, they're like the Jay-Z of the kitchen. They can do it all.

1 pound boneless, skinless chicken thighs (about 4 thighs)

1 tablespoon neutral oil, like canola

1 tablespoon Montreal steak seasoning

¾ teaspoon garlic powder

½ teaspoon kosher salt

½ teaspoon freshly ground black pepper

Preheat the oven to 375°F.

Toss the chicken thighs on a sheet pan with the oil, Montreal seasoning, garlic powder, salt, and pepper until evenly coated.

Roast in the oven until the chicken reaches an internal temperature of 165°F on an instant-read thermometer when inserted in the thickest part of the thigh, 12 to 15 minutes.

Remove the sheet pan from the oven and let the chicken cool in the pan for 10 to 15 minutes. Then transfer the chicken to a cutting board and cube the pieces. Use immediately, or place in a covered container and refrigerate for up to 2 days.

remix

SPICY PICKLE-BRINED ROASTED CHICKEN THIGHS: Put the chicken in a large bowl or other container and cover with the brine from a 32-ounce jar of pickled jalapeños, about 2 cups. Cover and chill in the fridge for 24 hours. Then drain the chicken and spread on the sheet pan. Instead of the garlic powder and Montreal seasoning, sub in 1 generous tablespoon of Chinese five-spice powder, then add the salt and pepper and toss the chicken to coat the pieces well. Add the oil, coating the chicken, then roast according to the directions. Cut into cubes, as directed.

DECEMBER 5, 1955—DECEMBER 20, 1956 The U.S. Supreme Court rules that segregation on public buses is unconstitutional after a pivotal thirteen-month mass protest of bus segregation policy in the Montgomery, Alabama, public transit system, known as the Montgomery Bus Boycott.[38]

1964 Fannie Lou Hamer, a Mississippi sharecropper and civil rights activist, organizes the Mississippi Freedom Democratic Party to elevate the voices of Black people within the Democratic Party. Hamer becomes instrumental in helping Black people register to vote and in organizing food cooperatives, as the founder of the Freedom Farm Cooperative.[39,40,41,42]

These days, you gotta have some veggie and vegan pizzas in your back pocket. And I don't mean as an afterthought, where you just take off the meat. Vegans want options as good as the carnivore choices. Some people want a slammin' veggie pizza just 'cuz they're in the mood for it. Some people can't eat dairy, but they still want to eat pizza.

Since my time cooking at Vedge—Philly's go-to vegan fine-dining spot—I've had a couple tricks up my sleeve. I started testing vegan pies the minute we planned Down North's menu. No surprise: melty cheese is the key. I tried all the vegan mozz's out there. Some parms, too. They all needed help melting, but the ones made with coconut milk melted best. That kind of vegan mozz is part of what makes our spicy vegan cheesesteak pie so fire. That, and the aji amarillo drizzle (see page 68). And the seasoned Sautéed Mushrooms (page 55). Grab a slice of P.S.K. (page 68), and you'll see what I mean.

Like all the Down North pies, these veggie and vegan pizzas have our signature Philly spin on the square pie: cheese on the dough and sauce on top, which is usually drizzled over the gooey cheese in a stylin' zigzag pattern after the pie is outta the oven. They're filling, too. One 10-inch pizza easily feeds two or three people. We have an in-store challenge for anyone who can eat a whole pie in a single sitting. Come check it out if you're in town.

—MIKE CARTER

MIKE CARTER

EXECUTIVE CHEF, DOWN NORTH

Before I wanted to be a gangster, I wanted to be a revolutionary.

Cooking is my happy place. To me, it's an art. I love being creative.

I've been around cooks my whole life. My grandfather was a butcher, a BBQ chef, and a truck driver (my family came up from the South, and back then you had to be a jack-of-all-trades). In the '70s, my grandpa's sister had a rib shack in West Philly, on 52nd Street. Everybody in our family worked there. Food and cooking are in my blood. One holiday, my grandfather asked me what I wanted to be when I grew up. I said I was gonna be a chef.

At age fourteen, though, I got pulled into the streets, and by the time I was sixteen, I caught a charge for armed robbery and home invasion. That sent me to the New Jersey Training School for Boys, run by the state's Juvenile Justice Commission. Even then, I always kept my eyes on the food prize; when I wasn't in class at the Burg, as we called it, I was in the kitchen tryin' to improve the food they fed us. Nobody likes plain oatmeal. I swiped the brown sugar and cinnamon from the Officer's Dining Hall to doctor it up. I took the paprika and garlic powder, too; the plain chicken they served us was garbage. (FTR, I always put those seasonings back.) Then, after being locked up there for thirty-two months, I got out and got my first catering job. At age nineteen, I enrolled in Philadelphia's Restaurant School at Walnut Hill. I was pursuing the chef dream.

But the streets have a way of pulling you back in. For guys like me, it's hard to see yourself making it anywhere *but* the streets. And when you're young, you make mistakes.

A year after I left the Burg, I caught another charge for aggravated assault with a deadly weapon. That charge got me locked up for seven and a half long years at SCI Greensburg, a Pennsylvania State Correctional Institution.

Most of those years, I cooked three meals a day for thousands of inmates, making things like grits, pancakes, Texas hash, chili, and spaghetti. As a cook, I had access to food, so my play was to sell five-pound bags of oatmeal for four-packs of Newports. You need money to survive in prison, and I was always working the food angles. That's where I made my very first pizza dough: crushed ramen noodles mixed with Cheez-Its in a potato chip bag. I topped it with commissary ingredients like beef summer sausage, kipper steaks, and sliced turkey logs, and I cooked the pizza in a bucket of electrified water in my jail cell. Check out the recipe on page 133.

When I got out, I was twenty-seven. First thing I did was start taking culinary classes at the Art Institute of Philadelphia. I saved up money for a food truck, too. Soon I had $15,000— I was keepin' that chef dream alive. Turned out I couldn't escape the carceral system, though. After a fire burnt down my grandma's house where I was living, I got a "technical" parole violation for failing to update my address.

That little slipup didn't send me back to jail, but a random cop stop did.

It happened like this: I was just rolling in University City with my man, Los. We were headed to the club, and we got pulled over for a damn taillight bein' out. Los told the cop straight up that he had a registered firearm in the car, and all Los's gun paperwork checked out. Still, the cop asked us to get out of the car. Knowing my priors and that technical violation, I ran.

Turns out, Los had another gun in the car—this one unregistered. When they caught me, they pinned that gun on me. As an ex-offender, I was an easy mark. The cop that got me said I moved back the passenger seat in Los's ride, and that's when they saw the unregistered gun. That was a damn lie because Los's electrical in the BMW didn't work. The cop also said Los gave him permission to search the car. Another lie.

People say recidivism is when someone comes out of prison, then re-offends and goes back to jail. But that ain't the whole truth. The U.S. incarceration system is a big business. It's the third largest employer in the country. It's like a hotel chain. They need people in them beds and a constant supply of offenders and re-offenders to keep the whole system running. Recidivism is part of a big-money business in law enforcement that recycles people like me back into the system.

This time when I got locked up, I went to prisons all over Pennsylvania, just waiting for my trumped-up gun charge to be tried in a court of law. It took twenty-seven months for that to happen. And every time my case came up, I'd get cuffed and shackled wrist to feet, and sent back to court, all for the judge just to postpone the case again, "pending officer's return to duty." Turns out, the original officer got shot in a different incident, and they wouldn't try my case without him being present.

Finally, I got in front of a Latina judge, who said to the prosecution, "Let me get this straight. You've had this man in jail for twenty-seven months pending officer's return because he had a technical parole violation, that only holds for six months, for an offense that happened back when he was twenty?"

She ended my case right then and there. No prosecution. That twenty-seven months was my shortest prison stay ever—but also the harshest. I missed the first two years of my daughter's life. And

that $15,000 I had saved for my food truck? It all went to pay lawyer fees.

When I came home after that, I threw myself into cooking. I catered, worked at Ruby Tuesday's, got a gig as the opening chef at a pizza place called Porta, and worked at Wiz Kid, Vedge, V Street, and Bernie's, in University City. I was committed to being a professional chef for good.

In early 2020, I got a call from a chef who needed an executive chef at this new pizza place called Down North. He said it would be run exclusively by formerly incarcerated people and would provide stable jobs, housing if we needed it, and free legal support. It was gonna be a place where we didn't have to hide our pasts—we could just be ourselves. Dope!

That summer I met Muhammad, Down North's founder, and I got to work on creating our now-signature and award-winning Philly-style square pizza. Dan "Pizza Gut" Gutter, who was a chef at Pizzeria Beddia and now Circles and Squares, showed me some love and taught me his square-pie dough. I played around with it. I wanted it lighter and fluffier, so I added more water. I couldn't afford the overnight fermentation, so I shortened it to a couple hours. For the cheese, I wanted more flavor, so I developed our own special mix. I took what the Gut showed me and made it my own.

That fall, Down North started doing pizza popups. Instead of just plain and pepperoni pies, I put people onto badass combos like beef bacon with caramelized pineapple, jalapeños, and BBQ sauce, our Flip Side (page 108). And, sautéed oyster and shiitake mushrooms with kale, red peppers, red onion, and Norf Sauce, our signature swicy-smoky tomato sauce, or what we call Uptown Vibes (page 66).

This is Philly pizza for the people—a better version of those rectangular slices from our youth. We named our pies after Philly rap songs that were meaningful to us, "Like What We Do" and "Yeah That's Us" (see page 16 for the playlist). The Down North menu reads like the soundtrack to our lives. When people come into the shop, the music, the flavors, and the good feelings bring people together like nothing else.

We opened in March 2021. Lines of hungry customers stretched out the door and down past the next street. From that day onward, we got featured in all the Philly media, as well as national spots—my pizza was voted "Best Square Pie" in *Philadelphia* magazine, and we had features in *Food & Wine*, the *New York Times*, *Forbes*, and *Eater*, plus on *NPR*, the *CBS Morning Show*—you name it.

In the fall, *Bon Appétit* magazine did a big spread called "Heads of the Table," profiling twelve restaurants that were changing the restaurant industry. My face and story were all on display: Michael Carter, former prison cook turned executive chef at the celebrated pizza restaurant, Down North.

The next day, Muhammad gets a call from my parole officer, saying, "We need Mike to come in."

I thought, *Are you fuckin' kidding me? I ain't been in a parole office for three years. I just got done reading about myself in* Bon Appétit; *now the law comes knocking on my door? That ain't no coincidence.*

They said they were auditing some old parole files and noticed I didn't complete a drug program back in 2017. But I was never convicted of any drug offense. My green sheet, which is like a to-do list when you get out of prison, was amended without my knowledge. Truth is, I think it was done out of spite. Here I am, running the busiest pizza spot in the city, and now I'm expected to do an outpatient drug program three times a week? I tell you, this is the carceral system doing what it does.

A week later, I was interviewed by Laura Benshoff on WHYY, our Philly NPR station. After talking about the Down North pizza and its mission, she asked about this thing with the drug program.

"So, you're telling me you might go back to jail if you don't complete this program?" I told her the ramifications if I didn't complete the program. Her response was, "I'm calling up Harrisburg."

The next day, my PO calls and says I don't have to complete the outpatient drug program. LFG! The case was finally closed and he texted me the "release from conditions" paper. The pen prevailed over the sword.

But I still don't get off parole until 2026, and I'll always be on pins and needles because any minor slipup could send me back inside. That's just how it is with guys like me. Parole and probation are the ugly cousins of the carceral system. Every year, 750,000 inmates get released from prison—but they need those people to come back in. Prisons don't get full funding unless they're at full capacity. Hard truth.

I believe nobody should be judged solely by their last mistake. That's why Down North's mission is front burner. We're trying to change the system. Before I wanted to be a gangster, I wanted to be a revolutionary, but ex-offenders can't attend protests about this shit. Police contact is a parole violation. So, Down North is my demonstration, showing what guys given a second chance can actually do. We're tryin' to break the cycle of kids going to juvie, then to jail, out on parole, then back to jail. We do it by employing formerly incarcerated people, serving great pizza, and building community (see page 187).

MAKES ONE
10-INCH
SQUARE PIE

NO
BETTA
LOVE

Our plain cheese pizza really shows off its "crown," the crusty cheese edge that forms all around the edges of the pizza. We call it "the fence" at Down North because we're all about combating prison recidivism. For the tallest fence, make sure you get the cheese to go all the way around the edges of the pan so it melts and crisps up. And remember, the sauce goes on top, not on the bottom. That's the square pie way. Get those two things right, and you'll know why we call this pizza No Betta Love.

¾ cup shredded low-moisture whole-milk mozzarella

¾ cup shredded provolone cheese

¾ cup shredded sharp white cheddar cheese

1 Down North Pizza Crust (page 30), parbaked in the pan

¾ cup Norf Sauce (page 34)

2 heaping tablespoons grated grana padano or parmesan cheese

Preheat the oven: If you have a pizza oven, preheat it to 700°F. In a home oven, set the temperature to 500° or 550°F, with the convection setting on if you have it, and put a baking stone or baking steel on the top oven rack set 6 to 8 inches below the heat. Preheat the oven for 1 hour.

Prep the pizza: In a medium bowl, mix the mozz, provolone, and cheddar cheeses. Spread the cheese mix evenly over the crust in the pan, and make sure it's pushed all the way to the edges. You want a good amount of cheese touching the pan to create a crispy "fence" all around the edges.

Bake: Slide the pan onto the baking stone or steel and cook until the edges of the pizza are dark brown, 10 to 15 minutes. In a home oven, if the edges aren't looking dark brown after 10 minutes, switch to the broiler setting. (With electric ovens, you may have to open the oven door for 10 seconds to make sure the broiler turns on.) Continue cooking for a few minutes until the pizza edges are dark brown but not burnt. Watch it like a hawk!

Slice and finish: Remove the pan from the oven and put it on a heatproof surface. Run a wide metal spatula around the edges of the pan to loosen the pizza, then use the spatula to pop out the pizza and move it to a cutting board. Let it cool for a minute, then slice into 6 pieces. Spoon big, wide (about 2 inches wide) diagonal stripes of Norf Sauce over the top, and finish with the grated cheese.

remix

VEGAN NO BETTA LOVE: Spread a thin layer of vegan mayo (a couple tablespoons) over the parbaked crust and replace the cheese mix with 2¼ cups shredded vegan mozzarella. For the finish, use 2 to 3 tablespoons grated vegan parmesan.

1964 The Student Nonviolent Coordinating Committee (SNCC) and the Congress of Racial Equality (CORE) mobilize northern college students to help register Black residents to vote in Mississippi's political system. The volunteer effort, known as Freedom Summer, is met with severe violent backlash and oppression from local officials and residents. Freedom Summer volunteers are beaten, assaulted, and murdered; and homes, businesses, and churches are burned and bombed.[43,44]

MAKES ONE
10-INCH
SQUARE PIE

UPTOWN VIBES

All pizza shops have their holy trinity of pies: plain cheese, pepperoni, and veggie. At Down North, that trinity is our No Betta Love (page 64), Roc the Mic (page 94), and this Uptown Vibes. I already had kale in the kitchen for our What We Do (page 96), and kale brings the green on this pie, too. Peppers and onions bring the red and purple. Add some mushrooms, and it's rockin'. At the Down North popups, this veggie pie took off like a viral tweet. Now it's a standard menu item.

1 or 2 large kale leaves (1 ounce), tough center stems removed

¾ cup shredded low-moisture whole-milk mozzarella

¾ cup shredded provolone cheese

¾ cup shredded sharp white cheddar cheese

1 Down North Pizza Crust (page 30), parbaked in the pan

¼ small red bell pepper, cored and thinly sliced

⅛ small red onion, thinly sliced

¾ cup Sautéed Mushrooms (page 55)

¾ cup Norf Sauce (page 34)

2 heaping tablespoons grated grana padano or parmesan cheese

Preheat the oven: If you have a pizza oven, preheat it to 700°F. In a home oven, set the temperature to 500° or 550°F, with the convection setting on if you have it, and put a baking stone or baking steel on the top rack of the oven set 6 to 8 inches below the heat. Preheat the oven for 1 hour.

Prep the pizza: Fill a large bowl with ice cubes and water. Bring a large pot of water to a boil, then drop in the kale leaves and cook until they're bright green, about 30 seconds or so. Remove with tongs or a slotted spoon and dunk the leaves in the ice water to stop the cooking. Then pluck out and set the kale aside on a paper towel to drain. When it's kinda dry, roughly chop the kale.

In a medium bowl, mix the mozz, provolone, and cheddar cheeses. Sprinkle the cheese blend evenly over the pizza crust in the pan. Make sure it's pushed all the way to the edges. You want a good amount of cheese touching the pan to create a crispy "fence" all around the edges. Layer on the pepper, onion, mushrooms, and kale.

Bake: Slide the pan onto the baking stone or steel and cook until the edges of the pizza are dark brown, 10 to 15 minutes. In a home oven, if the edges aren't looking dark brown after 10 minutes, switch on the broiler setting. (With electric ovens, you may have to open the oven door for 10 seconds to make sure the broiler turns on.) Continue cooking for a few minutes, until the pizza edges are dark brown but not burnt. Watch it like a hawk!

Slice and finish: Remove the pan from the oven and put it on a heatproof surface. Run a wide metal spatula around the edges of the pan to loosen the pizza, then use the spatula to pop out the pizza and move it to a cutting board. Let it cool for a minute, then slice into 6 pieces. Spoon big, wide (about 2 inches wide) diagonal stripes of Norf Sauce over the top. Finish with the grated cheese.

remix

VEGAN UPTOWN VIBES: Spread a thin layer of vegan mayo (a couple tablespoons) over the parbaked crust and replace the cheese mix with 2¼ cups shredded vegan mozzarella. For the finish, use 2 to 3 tablespoons grated vegan parmesan.

MARCH 7, 1965 Martin Luther King Jr. and other members of the Southern Christian Leadership Conference (SCLC), as well as John Lewis and other members of the Student Nonviolent Coordinating Committee (SNCC), march from Selma to Montgomery, Alabama, to peacefully protest political and police-led resistance to Black voting rights. As they peacefully cross the Edmund Pettus Bridge, marchers are met with police violence in a tragedy known as "Bloody Sunday."[45,46]

P.S.K.

Vegan cheesesteaks are a big thing in Philly. Our version uses mushrooms instead of meat and a sauce made from aji amarillo chiles for heat. I put Montreal seasoning on the mushrooms to give 'em a beefy taste. The inspiration for the sauce came from Vista Peru, a Peruvian joint on 2nd and Chestnut, in Philly. Their Peruvian chicken is so fire with that spicy yellow sauce. My take on the sauce adds a splash of flavor and color to the pizza. I drizzle the sauce on the pizza like it's a play on yellow Cheez Wiz, but spicy.

¼ cup vegan mayonnaise, plus a few tablespoons for the crust

1 tablespoon aji amarillo pepper paste

½ tablespoon Dijon mustard

Pinch of freshly ground black pepper

1 Down North Pizza Crust (page 30), parbaked in the pan

2 cups shredded vegan mozzarella

1 cup Sautéed Mushrooms (page 55)

¼ small red bell pepper, cored and thinly sliced

⅛ small red onion, thinly sliced

Preheat the oven: If you have a pizza oven, preheat it to 700°F. In a home oven, set the temperature to 500° or 550°F, with the convection setting on if you have it, and put a baking stone or baking steel on the top rack of the oven set 6 to 8 inches below the heat. Preheat the oven for 1 hour.

Make the aji amarillo drizzle: In a small bowl, whisk together the mayo, pepper paste, mustard, and black pepper. It should be squirtable, like sriracha; if it's too thick, add a little water. Then put it in a small squirt bottle (see page 23).

Prep the pizza: Spread a thin layer (a couple tablespoons) of mayo over the crust in the pan, then spread the vegan mozz evenly over the mayo, making sure it's pushed to the edges. You want a good amount of cheese touching the pan to create a crispy "fence" all around the edges. Cover the entire pie with the mushrooms, bell pepper, and red onion.

Bake: Slide the pan onto the baking stone or steel and cook until the edges of the pizza are dark brown, 10 to 15 minutes. In a home oven, if the edges aren't looking dark brown after 10 minutes, switch to the broiler setting. (With electric ovens, you may have to open the oven door for 10 seconds to make sure the broiler turns on.) Continue cooking for a few minutes, until the pizza edges are dark brown but not burnt. Watch it like a hawk!

Slice and finish: Remove the pan from the oven and put it on a heatproof surface. Run a wide metal spatula around the edges of the pan to loosen the pizza, then use the spatula to pop out the pizza and move it to a cutting board. Let it cool for a minute, then slice into 6 pieces. Drizzle on the aji amarillo sauce in a bad-ass zigzag, then dig in.

JULY 10, 1964 In Jonesboro, Louisiana, a group of Black men form the Deacons of Defense and Justice to protect Congress of Racial Equity (CORE) members from Ku Klux Klan violence.[47]

1966 The Black Panther Party is formed.[48]

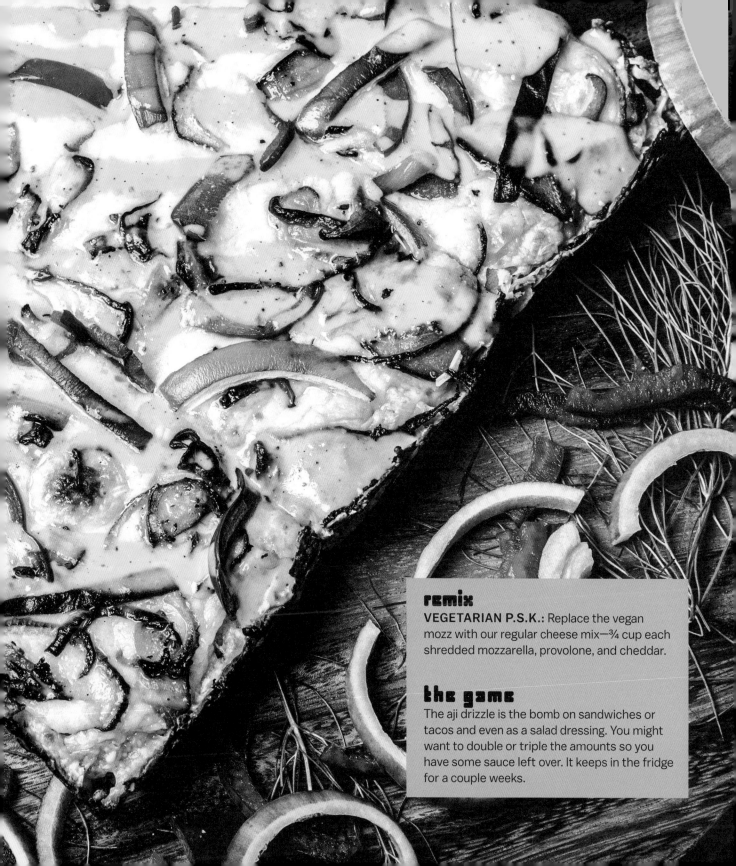

remix

VEGETARIAN P.S.K.: Replace the vegan mozz with our regular cheese mix—¾ cup each shredded mozzarella, provolone, and cheddar.

the game

The aji drizzle is the bomb on sandwiches or tacos and even as a salad dressing. You might want to double or triple the amounts so you have some sauce left over. It keeps in the fridge for a couple weeks.

SUMMER–TIME

State Road, in northeast Philly, has four city-run prisons. In 2014, they broke ground on the Philadelphia Prison Orchard behind the PICC (Philadelphia Institutional Correctional Center). It has two acres of fruit trees, shrubs, and vines, including apple, pear, and fig trees; raspberry bushes; and kiwi and grape vines. The orchard was supposed to provide fresh food for prison kitchens while helping train guys like me for farming and landscaping jobs. But none of that food ever went inside the prison walls. Instead, the fruit went to food pantries and the city just got free labor. When Covid hit, no one tended the orchards, and the fruit withered on the vine.

Later in 2020, Muhammad and I started working with PICC to get things growing again. I also planted stuff I wanted to use at the restaurant. We tried to get the orchard produce into the prison commissary, but the powers that be wouldn't allow it. The next summer, I came back to the shop with these big-ass boxes of produce and the best cherry tomatoes I'd ever grown. I pan-roasted the tomatoes, blended up a quick basil pesto, and put 'em both on a pie with some roasted red peppers. Taste it and tell me that's not the perfect summertime pizza!

JULY 28, 1967 President Lyndon B. Johnson establishes the Kerner Commission to understand civil rights uprisings occurring across the country. The Commission finds the roots of unrest include unemployment, housing, police brutality, and inadequate social services.[49,50]

1 tablespoon olive oil

About 8 cherry or grape tomatoes, halved

¾ cup shredded low-moisture whole-milk mozzarella

¾ cup shredded provolone cheese

¾ cup shredded sharp white cheddar cheese

¼ cup Basil Pesto (page 44)

1 Down North Pizza Crust (page 30), parbaked in the pan

About 6 good-looking whole, fresh basil leaves

½ cup roasted red pepper strips

2 heaping tablespoons grated grana padano or parmesan cheese

Preheat the oven: If you have a pizza oven, preheat it to 700°F. In a home oven, set the temperature to 500° or 550°F, with the convection setting on if you have it, and put a baking stone or baking steel on a top rack of the oven set 6 to 8 inches below the heat. Preheat the oven for 1 hour.

Pan-roast the tomatoes: Heat a medium skillet over medium-high heat, then add the olive oil. When it is shimmering, toss in the tomatoes and cook until they get a little charred here and there, 3 to 4 minutes. Shake the pan now and then for even cooking.

Prep the pizza: In a medium bowl, mix the mozz, provolone, and cheddar cheeses. Spread the pesto evenly over the parbaked crust in the pan. Lay the fresh basil leaves over the pesto, then sprinkle the cheese mix over the top. (That way you'll see the basil outlines when the cheese melts.) Make sure the cheese is pushed to the edges, too. You want a good amount of cheese touching the pan to create a crispy "fence" all around the edges. Evenly scatter the red pepper and then the pan-roasted tomatoes over the cheese.

Bake: Slide the pan onto the baking stone or steel and cook until the edges of the pizza are dark brown, 10 to 15 minutes. In a home oven, if the edges aren't looking dark brown after 10 minutes, switch on the broiler setting. (With electric ovens, you may have to open the oven door for 10 seconds to make sure the broiler turns on.) Continue cooking for a few minutes, until the pizza edges are dark brown but not burnt. Watch it like a hawk!

Slice and finish: Remove the pan from the oven and put it on a heatproof surface. Run a wide metal spatula around the edges of the pan to loosen the pizza, then use the spatula to pop out the pizza and move it to a cutting board. Let it cool for a minute, then slice into 6 pieces. Finish with the grated cheese.

remix

VEGAN SUMMERTIME: Spread a thin layer of vegan mayo (a couple tablespoons) over the parbaked crust and replace the cheese mix with 2¼ cups shredded vegan mozzarella. For the finish, use 2 to 3 tablespoons grated vegan parmesan.

TWO FIFTEEN

Philly's area code is 215, and after the Eagles lost the Super Bowl in 2023, I had to give our city some love. This pie's an ode to the real Philly sandwich: not a cheesesteak, but roast pork with broccoli rabe and sharp provolone. We don't do pork at Down North, so I use pickle-brined mushrooms (heads up—they marinate overnight). Lots of people get Italian long hots on their roast pork sandwich to spice it up, so I took that idea and made a long-hot gravy that's spooned on top of this pie. Here you get all those Philly roast pork sandwich vibes with a veg twist.

5 ounces fresh oyster mushrooms, tough ends trimmed

About 1 cup pickle brine (from a jar of pickles)

About 3 tablespoons neutral oil, such as canola

3 Italian green long hot peppers (or shishito peppers, see The Game)

2 tablespoons unsalted butter

4 medium garlic cloves, minced

¼ cup all-purpose flour

Marinate the mushrooms: Separate the mushrooms into individual pieces, then place in a medium bowl and add the pickle brine. Cover the bowl with plastic and marinate overnight in the refrigerator.

Preheat the oven: If you have a pizza oven, preheat it to 700°F. In a home oven, set the temperature to 500° or 550°F, with the convection setting on if you have it, and put a baking stone or baking steel on a top rack of the oven set 6 to 8 inches below the heat. Preheat the oven for 1 hour.

Make the long-hot gravy: Heat a medium skillet over medium-high heat. Add a few teaspoons of the oil. When the oil is shimmering, add the long hots and sear until lightly charred all over, 4 to 5 minutes, tossing a few times. Set one pepper aside for a garnish. Let the other two peppers cool a bit, then trim the stems and remove the ribs and seeds. Chop the flesh and set aside.

Melt the butter in a small saucepan over medium heat, then add half the garlic, shaking the pan to coat the garlic with butter. In 2 to 3 minutes, just before the garlic starts to brown, stir in the flour until moistened. Shake the pan to spread out the flour, then let it cook 1 minute. Whisk in the broth and simmer until the gravy thickens, 3 to 4 minutes.

Transfer the mix to a blender or use a stick blender in the saucepan, add the chopped long hots, and blend until the sauce is all silky smooth. Taste it, and season to taste with the salt and pepper. The gravy should be thin enough to drizzle; if it's too thick, add a little more broth.

¾ cup vegetable broth, plus more if needed

About ½ teaspoon kosher salt

About ¼ teaspoon freshly ground black pepper

2 to 4 stems broccoli rabe (about 4 ounces total), tough ends trimmed

¾ cup shredded low-moisture whole-milk mozzarella

¾ cup shredded provolone cheese

¾ cup shredded sharp white cheddar cheese

1 Down North Pizza Crust (page 30), parbaked in the pan

2 heaping tablespoons grated grana padano or parmesan cheese

the game

Shishito peppers are a little smaller and milder than long hots, so use a few more and add some red pepper flakes along with the broth.

Drizzle any leftover gravy over fries or a fried egg. It's baller on halal beef sausage (see page 23).

Sear the mushrooms: Place a medium skillet over high heat and add about a tablespoon of oil. Drain the marinade from the mushrooms, pat 'em dry, and when the oil is shimmering, add the mushrooms and cook until they start just to brown a little but are still meaty and juicy, 3 to 4 minutes, stirring occasionally. Remove from the heat and set aside.

Blanch and sauté the rabe: Fill a large bowl with ice cubes and water. Bring a large saucepan of salted water to a boil, add the broccoli rabe, and blanch for 30 seconds. Using tongs, transfer the rabe to the ice water to stop the cooking. After about 30 seconds, remove the rabe from the ice water and pat dry with paper towels, then cut into 1-inch pieces.

Heat the same skillet over medium heat, swirl in another tablespoon of oil, then add the broccoli rabe and sauté until it's almost tender, about 5 minutes, stirring now and then. Add the remaining garlic and cook for another minute (don't burn the garlic!).

Prep the pizza: In a medium bowl, mix the mozz, provolone, and cheddar cheeses. Scatter the cheese blend evenly over the parbaked crust in the pan. Make sure it's pushed to the edges. You want a good amount of cheese touching the pan to create a crispy "fence" all around the edges. Distribute the mushrooms and rabe over the top.

Bake: Slide the pan onto the baking stone or steel and cook until the edges of the pizza are dark brown, 10 to 15 minutes. In a home oven, if the edges aren't looking dark brown after 10 minutes, switch to the broiler setting. (With electric ovens, you may have to open the oven door for 10 seconds to make sure the broiler turns on.) Continue cooking for a few minutes, until the pizza edges are dark brown but not burnt. Watch it like a hawk!

Slice and finish: Remove the pan from the oven and put it on a heatproof surface. Run a wide metal spatula around the edges of the pan to loosen the pizza, then use the spatula to pop out the pizza and move it to a cutting board. Let it cool for a minute, then slice into 6 pieces. Drizzle a generous ¼ cup of the long-hot gravy in a diagonal zigzag over the top. Finish with the grated cheese and place the reserved long-hot pepper upright on top.

remix

VEGAN TWOFIFTEEN: For the long-hot gravy, use vegan butter instead of dairy butter, and if you can find it, vegan no-chicken broth instead of vegetable broth (it's got more flavor). Spread a thin layer of vegan mayo (a couple tablespoons) over the parbaked crust, add the topping, and replace the cheese mix with 2¼ cups shredded vegan mozzarella. For the finish, use 2 to 3 tablespoons grated vegan parmesan.

1968 The American Indian Movement (AIM) is founded in Minneapolis, Minnesota, to organize against unemployment, substandard and slum housing, and racial discrimination impacting the Native American community. Their efforts also involve reclamation of tribal land and treaty rights. The Federal Bureau of Investigation (FBI) and the Central Intelligence Agency (CIA) confront and suppress AIM leadership and efforts starting in the early 1970s, culminating in a brutal confrontation at Wounded Knee, South Dakota, in February 1973.[51,52]

SARA SMILE

I came up with this vegan pizza while testing a vegan hoagie that's on the menu at our new restaurant, Out West. It's a pastrami sandwich situation, done vegan. To stand in for the beef, we boil beets, get 'em smoked and charred on the mini grill we have on our patio, and then marinate them overnight in seasoned oil. Once you cut 'em thin, those red beet rounds look like cured meat on pizza. The Thousand Island dressing sends it. Drizzle it over the top and the orange color pops so good off the red beets and the white cheese.

2 to 3 small red beets (about 12 ounces), trimmed

½ large white onion

½ cup extra-virgin olive oil

2 generous tablespoons sherry vinegar

½ tablespoon Dijon mustard

½ tablespoon Montreal steak seasoning

1 teaspoon dried oregano

1 teaspoon kosher salt

2 cups shredded vegan mozzarella

1 Down North Pizza Crust (page 30), parbaked in the pan

¼ cup Vegan Thousand Island Dressing (page 51)

A few sprigs of fresh dill, chopped, for garnish

Boil, smoke, and marinate the beets: First, put on some hip-hop music; then, bring a large saucepan of water to a boil. Drop in the beets and simmer until they're tender when poked with a knife and the skin looks like it's loosening up, 20 to 25 minutes. Drain, let the beets cool a bit, then peel. (You could drop them in ice water if you don't want to wait for them to cool down, but the skins come off easiest while they're still warm; wear gloves if you worry about staining your hands. And if you want to skip this whole process, just buy already boiled and peeled beets from the supermarket.)

If you are using a charcoal grill, fire it up to medium-high heat, with all the coals banked to one side. Put a handful of wood chunks or chips on the hot coals. If you are using a gas grill, just light the burners on one side only and wrap wood chips in a flat packet of aluminum foil. Poke a bunch of holes in the packet, then place it over a lit burner beneath the grill grate.

Place the peeled beets on the unheated side of the grill, opposite the smoking wood. Cover and let the beets smoke for about 15 minutes. Then move the beets directly over the heat to get some char on them, about 10 minutes total, turning now and then for even charring. (If you want to skip this whole process, briefly smoke the cooked and peeled beets on the stovetop (see The Game).

Thinly slice the onion on a mandoline. We're talkin' paper thin. (If you can do that with a knife, great. Slice the beets the same way.) In a medium bowl, whisk together the olive oil, vinegar, mustard, steak seasoning, oregano, and salt. Add the beets and onion, and massage to coat everything nice and even (use gloves, if you've got them). Massage gently to make sure the beet rounds stay intact; they should look kinda like salami slices. Cover the bowl with plastic and marinate at room temperature for at least 8 hours or up to 24 hours. Drain the beets and onion and set aside.

Preheat the oven: If you have a pizza oven, preheat it to 700°F. In a home oven, set the temperature to 500° or 550°F, with the convection setting on if you have it, and put a baking stone or baking steel on a top rack of the oven set 6 to 8 inches below the heat. Preheat the oven for 1 hour.

Prep the pizza: Spread the vegan mozz evenly over the parbaked crust in the pan, and make sure it's pushed to the edges. You want a good amount of cheese touching the pan to create a crispy "fence" all around the edges. Cover the entire pie with about 1 cup of the marinated beets and onion, laying down some onion first, then the beet circles close together in a single layer so it looks like pepperoni slices.

Bake: Slide the pan onto the baking stone or steel and cook until the edges of the pizza are dark brown, 10 to 15 minutes. In a home oven, if the edges aren't looking dark brown after 10 minutes, switch on the broiler setting. (With electric ovens, you may have to open the oven door for 10 seconds to make sure the broiler turns on.) Continue cooking for a few minutes, until the pizza edges are dark brown but not burnt. Watch it like a hawk!

Slice and finish: Remove the pan from the oven and put it on a heatproof surface. Run a wide metal spatula around the edges of the pan to loosen the pizza, then use the spatula to pop out the pizza and move it to a cutting board. Let it cool for a minute, then slice into 6 pieces. Drizzle on the dressing and garnish with a sprinkling of the fresh dill.

the game

If you don't have a smoker, you can cheat and smoke the beets on the stovetop. It won't be quite as good, but it'll be good. Open a window or turn on your hood vent. Find a metal colander or perforated pan or steamer basket that will fit into a medium saucepan. Line the saucepan with foil and a handful of small wood chips. Cover with a lid or foil, and turn the heat to high, watching it until you see smoke coming from the pan, 3 to 4 minutes. Put the beets in the colander (or pan or basket), put the colander in the saucepan, and cover with the lid or foil. Cut the heat to medium and let the beets be infused with smoke for 10 to 15 minutes. Let cool briefly, then disassemble and set the beets aside.

DECEMBER 4, 1969 The Chicago Police Department and the Federal Bureau of Investigation (FBI) collaborate to murder Black Panther Party leader Fred Hampton. Hampton led the Rainbow Coalition, a seminal mobilization of Black Panther Party members, the Young Lords Organization, and the Young Patriots. The Rainbow Coalition brought Black, Latinx, and White social-justice advocates together to form an alliance that transcended their racial and ethnic classifications.[53,54]

HONCHO'S BIRTHDAY PIE

In November 2021, we were hurtin' for people to work at the shop. Muhammad had to fill in—even on his birthday. For lunch most days he usually just grabs a salad, so I got to thinkin': the guy who takes care of everyone else rarely gets taken care of. So, I made him a pizza. An hour before service, I ran out to get some arugula. We had some grape tomatoes on hand, and I sent Myles to the corner store for birthday candles. Muhammad doesn't do dairy, so I pulled out our vegan mozz and made a vegan Caesar dressing for the arugula. With our sautéed mushrooms, the pizza was shaping up to be a solid on-the-fly vegan pie. Muhammad came in on his birthday, tied on his apron, and was about to bag up a customer's food when I walked toward him with the pizza, with the candles all lit up, grinning cheek to cheek. Myles was laughing, back by the fryer. I made the head honcho take a break and sit down for a proper lunch. He fucked that pizza *up*.

2 cups shredded vegan mozzarella

1 Down North Pizza Crust (page 30), parbaked in the pan

1 cup Sautéed Mushrooms (page 55)

5 cherry or grape tomatoes, halved

1 cup fresh arugula

About 3 tablespoons Vegan Caesar Dressing (page 50)

¾ cup Norf Sauce (page 34)

2½ tablespoons grated vegan parmesan cheese

Cracked black peppercorns

Preheat the oven: If you have a pizza oven, preheat it to 700°F. In a home oven, set the temperature to 500° or 550°F, with the convection setting on if you have it, and put a baking stone or baking steel on a top rack of the oven set 6 to 8 inches below the heat. Preheat the oven for 1 hour.

Prep the pizza: Spread the vegan mozz evenly over the crust in the pan, and make sure it's pushed to the edges. You want a good amount of cheese touching the pan to create a crispy "fence" all around the edges. Top with the sautéed mushrooms.

Bake: Slide the pan onto the baking stone or steel and cook until the edges of the pizza are dark brown, 10 to 15 minutes. In a home oven, if the edges aren't looking dark brown after 10 minutes, switch on the broiler setting. (With electric ovens, you may have to open the oven door for 10 seconds to make sure the broiler turns on.) Continue cooking for a few minutes, until the pizza edges are dark brown but not burnt. Watch it like a hawk!

Prep the topping: In a medium bowl, toss the tomatoes with the arugula and about 3 tablespoons of the dressing.

Slice and finish: Remove the pan from the oven and put it on a heatproof surface. Run a wide metal spatula around the edges of the pan to loosen the pizza, then use the spatula to pop out the pizza and move it to a cutting board. Let it cool for a minute, then slice into 6 pieces. Spoon big diagonal stripes (each about 2 inches wide) of the Norf Sauce over the pizza. Scatter the salad over the top and finish with the grated cheese and some black pepper.

1969—1980 The Black Panther Party's Free Breakfast Program is initiated to solve the problem of children going to school hungry, complicating their ability to learn and focus. The program starts at St. Augustine Church in Oakland, California, with 11 children fed on the inaugural day and increases to 135 children by the end of the week. The Free Breakfast Program is considered one of the most seminal initiatives of the Black Panther Party's Survival Programs.[55,56]

STREETS OF PHILADELPHIA

Triple Bottom Brewing is a Philly brewery that hires formerly incarcerated people, so they're like our brothers. I've been doing pizzas there since we opened Down North, and every year they have a big anniversary party. One year, the cooler weather was comin' in and I was craving potato-leek soup. The idea came like lightning: a lemony potato-leek pizza with a drizzle of creamy leek puree, some fresh chives, and funky grated cheese. Plus, a bacon crumble on top—optional, but strongly recommended 'cuz bacon and potatoes are a home run.

4 strips beef bacon (optional)

1 medium leek (about 8 ounces), root end and top 1 inch of green trimmed, then halved lengthwise and washed

Extra-virgin olive oil (see The Game)

Kosher salt and freshly ground black pepper

1 cup sour cream

Juice of 1 lemon

3 medium waxy white potatoes (about 1 pound), very thinly sliced with a mandoline or knife

¾ cup shredded low-moisture whole-milk mozzarella

¾ cup shredded provolone cheese

¾ cup shredded sharp white cheddar cheese

1 Down North Pizza Crust (page 30), parbaked in the pan

1 tablespoon chopped fresh chives

2 to 3 tablespoons grated Ogleshield or Gruyère cheese (see The Game)

Crisp the bacon (if using): Preheat the oven to 350°F. Lay out the bacon strips on a rack in a small sheet pan and bake until nice and crisp, 15 to 20 minutes. Drain the bacon on paper towels, saving any fat for another use (it keeps for months in a covered container in the fridge). When the bacon is cool, crumble the strips or break into smaller pieces, and set aside.

Prep the leek: Keep the oven set at 350°F or preheat to that temperature. Cut the cleaned leek in half crosswise where the white part meets the green. Thinly slice the white bottom crosswise and toss into a small sheet pan. Drizzle with about a tablespoon of olive oil, and season with about ¼ teaspoon each of salt and pepper. Use your hands to get the leek pieces evenly coated, then shake the pan so they lay out in an even layer. Bake until the leek pieces soften and cook down a bit, about 15 minutes. They should be only a little brown at the edges. Remove and set aside.

Meanwhile, fill a small bowl with ice cubes and water. Bring a medium pot of water to a boil and drop in the green leek top pieces until they're blanched bright green, 30 seconds or so. Remove with tongs or a slotted spoon and drop into the ice water to stop the cooking. When cold, remove and dry on a kitchen towel.

Put the blanched leek green pieces in a blender along with the sour cream, half the lemon juice, about 2 tablespoons of olive oil, and a big pinch each of salt and pepper. Blend until smooth—it should be the consistency of ranch dressing. Pour the creamy leek puree into a squeeze bottle and set aside or chill until ready to use.

Prep the potatoes: Keep the oven set at 350°F or preheat to that temperature. Spread out the potato slices in a big sheet pan and drizzle with a couple tablespoons of olive oil, about 1 teaspoon of salt, and ½ teaspoon of pepper. Drizzle with the rest of the lemon juice, then massage all that flavor into the potato slices with your hands. Make sure they're good and coated, and are evenly spaced in the pan. Bake until the slices are cooked about halfway through, 15 to 20 minutes. The potatoes should be tender but not so soft they fall apart. (They'll cook a little more on the pizza.) Remove and let cool.

Preheat the oven: If you have a pizza oven, preheat it to 700°F. In a home oven, set the temperature to 500° or 550°F, with the convection setting on if you have it, and put a baking stone or baking steel on a top rack of the oven set 6 to 8 inches below the heat. Preheat the oven for 1 hour.

1970 President Richard M. Nixon signs the Controlled Substances Act, which creates a drug classification system, with marijuana included in the most dangerous category. In 1971, Nixon declares a "War on Drugs" before the Washington press corps.[57,58,59]

Prep the pizza: In a large bowl, mix the mozz, provolone, and cheddar cheeses with the leek white pieces. Sprinkle the mixture evenly over the crust in the pan. Make sure it's pushed all the way to the edges. You want a good amount of cheese touching the pan to create a crispy "fence" all around the edges. Shingle the potato slices over the top.

Bake: Slide the pan onto the baking stone or steel and cook until the potatoes are fully cooked and lightly browned and the edges of the pizza are dark brown, 10 to 15 minutes. In a home oven, if the edges aren't looking dark brown after 10 minutes, switch on the broiler setting. (With electric ovens, you may have to open the oven door for 10 seconds to make sure the broiler turns on.) Continue cooking for a few minutes, until the pizza edges are dark brown but not burnt. Watch it like a hawk!

Slice and finish: Remove the pizza pan from the oven and put it on a heatproof surface. Run a wide metal spatula around the edges of the pan to loosen the pizza, then use the spatula to pop out the pizza and move it to a cutting board. Let it cool for a minute, then slice into 6 pieces. Squeeze the green leek puree in a zigzag pattern over the pie and top with the crumbled bacon (if using) and the chopped chives. Sprinkle the grated cheese over the top and have at it. This pie's a carb-lover's dream!

remix

VEGAN STREETS OF PHILADELPHIA: Use vegan bacon and cook it until crisp so you can crumble it. Use vegan sour cream, too. Spread a thin layer of vegan mayo (a couple tablespoons) over the parbaked crust and replace the cheese mix with 2¼ cups shredded vegan mozzarella. In a small bowl, mix the cooked leek white pieces into the vegan mozz and spread the mozz-leek mix over the crust all the way to the edges. For the finish, use 2 to 3 tablespoons grated vegan parmesan.

the game

I love lemony potatoes. If you want this pizza extra bright and lemony, use lemon-infused olive oil instead of regular extra-virgin olive oil.

Ogleshield is a buttery-rich semi-hard cheese that melts well and has a little onion flavor. If you can't find it, go with another good melter that pairs with potatoes, like Gruyère.

You'll have some creamy leek puree left over; drizzle it on french fries or use it as a creamy salad dressing. It'll keep for about a week in the fridge.

Old-school pizzaiolos will say you can't put chicken on pizza. You can't put pineapple on pizza. At Down North, we're not hampered by these traditions. We love American-style pizza, and that opens the door to all kinds of topping combos. Like a spicy bacon BBQ pineapple pizza (see page 108), a lamb sausage white pizza with lemon ricotta, za'atar, and garlic honey drizzle (see page 105), and yes, even a cheesesteak pizza (see page 114).

My philosophy is that any meat you might cook and serve with bread and/or cheese, you can just put on pizza and serve as a single item. Take smoked brisket. It's often served with white sandwich bread. It's even better with cheese on pizza (see page 117). Cheesesteak: fantastic as pizza. Seasoned ground beef: with taco seasoning, it makes a damn fine pizza (see page 120). BBQ chicken: that's an easy one. BBQ chicken pizza is getting more common these days. We make ours with pepperoncini and red onion (see page 103).

Notice that we don't do pork. Our shop is halal, so we use beef pepperoni and beef sausage on pizzas. And yeah, even though our pepperoni pizza, Roc the Mic (page 94), is our top seller, we think you'll really dig our Thai curry chicken pizza (see page 124) and our crab fry pizza (see page 128), too!

—MIKE CARTER

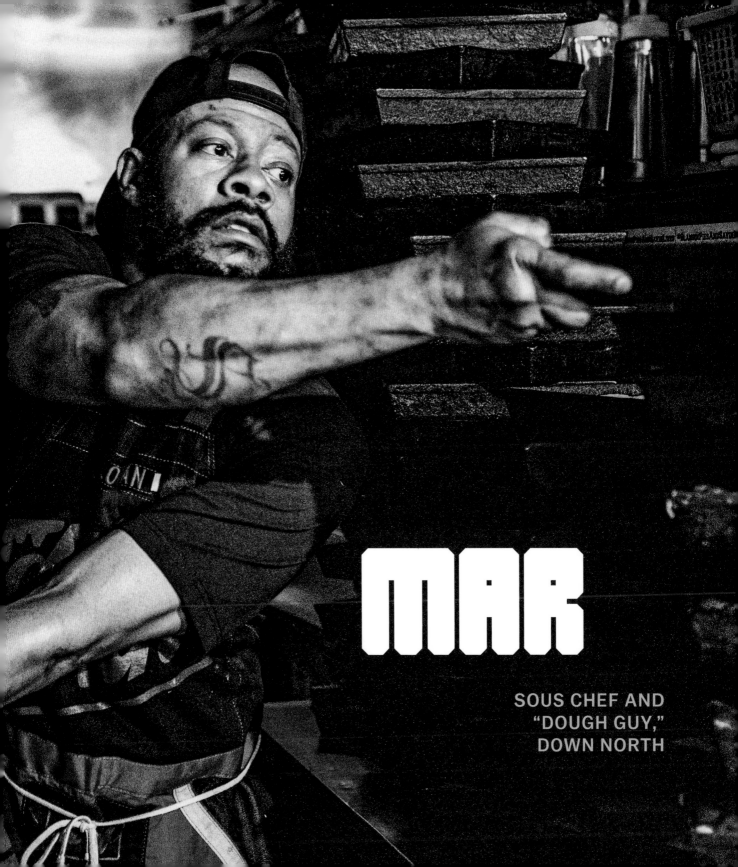

MAR

SOUS CHEF AND
"DOUGH GUY,"
DOWN NORTH

We're all at Down North for the mission: slangin' pies and savin' lives. It's for the kids. My kids, chef Mike's kids, the neighborhood kids . . . all of 'em. We wanna make sure our kids don't start goin' down the same paths we did, havin' the same troubles we had. There's always a solution. There's always a way out. I lost twenty-seven friends to the streets while I was in prison. It doesn't have to be that way.

My mother had me when she was only fourteen. She was just a kid with a kid, tryin' to make ends meet. She used to rob the local store so we'd have food to eat; when I was nine years old, cops came to our door and five police officers threw her to the ground. I tried to help her, then I got slammed down. Knocked unconscious. When I woke up, my mother was gone and I was alone. That was my first brush with the police.

This was in the Wilson Park Project, in South Philly. Everybody there had experiences like this. I got my first court case when I was twelve. I didn't commit the crime, but it didn't matter—I was running with the guys who did. And in high school, everybody gets labeled and you don't know any better, so you start leaning into the label. It becomes who you think you are.

I started hustling, doing what I had to do to survive in the city. By the time I was seventeen, I was selling drugs up at Penn State, in Altoona, Pa. I was up there so much I had a serious girlfriend there. I told her my name was Romeo, I was on a basketball team, and we were playing tournaments in town. I didn't tell her my real name 'cuz I didn't want her to know I was hustling and scare her off. The same day she finds out she's pregnant, I got arrested for possession.

I was coming out of a parking lot, and the Altoona cops pulled me over. I didn't have a driver's license, so they were allowed to search the vehicle. They found crack cocaine under my seat. I said the car was a rental and the drugs must've already been there. They brought me down to the station, stripped me, and found a big wad of money. That was that. I got charged and convicted for violation of the Controlled Substances Act, criminal use of a communication facility, possession with intent to deliver, and four other criminal offenses. I got eight different convictions for one illegal activity: selling drugs with a cell phone.

My girlfriend came to visit me at Blair County Prison and told me she was pregnant. I didn't get to meet our son, Shamarr, until I got out of prison four years later. I did everything I could to get out of there. I mean, all the right things. I enrolled in the tech training program to

I lost twenty-seven friends to the streets while I was

get some electrician skills, I joined the basketball team (we brought two championships to the jail), and I tried to be eligible for every program they had. I even got a scholarship.

My motive was to see my son, Shamarr. I missed his first bite. His first words. I never met my dad, and I didn't want to be that kind of dad. I wanted to be there for my son.

When I came home, I was twenty-three, and seeing my son was the turning point. I did whatever I could to stay off the streets. When you're in prison, you learn how to cook food in your cell, so I figured I could go off that. My first restaurant job was at Fox and Hound, on 15th and Spruce, in Philadelphia. I started mopping floors and ended up making cheesesteaks. At Fadó Irish Pub, I learned all the kitchen basics: sanitation, safety, knife cuts, and how to lead a crew. I cooked pasta at the Hard Rock Café in Center City, learned French food at Urban Farmer, and eventually became sous chef at Bernie's in University City. That's where I met Miz (Mike Carter).

When the pandemic hit, I did some catering and popups, and Miz was at all of them. Captain Mike had my back. That fall, Miz started doing his own popups at this place called Down North Pizza. I showed up at his popups, and he was running around like a madman, a one-man show. I said, "Want me to jump on that dough for you?" "Yeah," he goes, "you rock that out."

At first, I didn't have any intention of staying—truth be told, I don't even like pizza. But Miz was my brother and I wanted to support. Now I'm the dough guy at Down North. We're able to be ourselves here. Everyone is on the same playing field. I can joke. Laugh. Speak freely.

Down North has impacted me personally in a big way. Hamm (Muhammad) is a giver, and he saw an opportunity for me to give back to my Wilson Park neighborhood. Hamm and Down North helped raise $20,000 so we could provide Christmas to single mothers who couldn't do it on their own. I never had Christmas as a kid, so this hit deep for me. I was able to pass out $2,000 envelopes to ten families in my community. We went to Walmart for Christmas, and you'd think people were buying TVs and shit. No, they were buying food. Clothes for their children. Necessities. One mother bought an air mattress 'cuz her kids didn't have beds.

Making the dough, livin' out the mission at Down North . . . this place helped me find my purpose. I found a home here, and I can't see myself doing nothing else. I got offers, but no one does it like Down North.

ROC THE MIC

You couldn't go anywhere in the early 2000s without hearing "Roc the Mic." That song is iconic and a Philly pride thing—one of the hottest raps on Jay-Z's Roc-A-Fella Records. I've been in Baltimore, Jersey City, and New York, and when that song comes on, everybody starts doin' the dance from the video. Even now, Philly DJs will bust it out at block parties. It's like pepperoni pizza—everybody's favorite. Perfect fit for this pie. It's a straight-up pepperoni pizza with our signature spicy-sweet tomato sauce and grated parm for garnish. We use beef pepperoni 'cuz a lot of people in North Philly don't eat pork. Hell, a lot of people across the country don't eat pork. Even the rappers on that song don't.

¾ cup shredded low-moisture whole-milk mozzarella

¾ cup shredded provolone cheese

¾ cup shredded sharp white cheddar cheese

1 Down North Pizza Crust (page 30), parbaked in the pan

36 thin slices halal beef pepperoni (about 3 ounces)

¾ cup Norf Sauce (page 34)

2 heaping tablespoons grated grana padano or parmesan cheese

Preheat the oven: If you have a pizza oven, preheat it to 700°F. In a home oven, set the temperature to 500° or 550°F, with the convection setting on if you have it, and put a baking stone or baking steel on a top rack of the oven set 6 to 8 inches below the heat. Preheat the oven for 1 hour.

Prep the pizza: In a medium bowl, mix the mozz, provolone, and cheddar cheeses. Spread the cheese mix evenly over the crust in the pan, and make sure it's pushed all the way to the edges. You want a good amount of cheese touching the pan to create a crispy "fence" all around the edges. Cover the pizza with the pepperoni to make 6 rows of 6 slices each. You should barely be able to see the cheese underneath.

Bake: Put the pan on the baking stone or steel and cook until the edges of the pizza are dark brown, 10 to 15 minutes. In a home oven, if the edges aren't looking dark brown after 10 minutes, switch on the broiler setting. (With electric ovens, you may have to open the oven door for 10 seconds to make sure the broiler turns on.) Continue cooking for a few minutes, until the pizza edges are dark brown but not burnt. Watch it like a hawk!

Slice and finish: Remove the pan from the oven and put it on a heatproof surface. Run a wide metal spatula around the edges of the pan to loosen the pizza, then use the spatula to pop out the pizza and move it to a cutting board. Let it cool for a minute, then slice into 6 pieces. Spoon big, wide (about 2 inches wide) diagonal stripes of the Norf Sauce over the top and finish with the grated cheese.

SEPTEMBER 9, 1971 In upstate New York's Attica Prison, incarcerated people, 54 percent of whom are Black, protest harsh conditions of confinement and management of human bodies. The Attica Prison Riot becomes one of the most consequential prison uprisings since the Civil War, as the 1970s mark the beginning of mass incarceration while civil rights activism is criminalized. Prison populations expand as the Southern Strategy is deployed to increase political support among white voters by appealing to racism against African Americans.[60,61,62,63,64]

remix

VEGAN ROC THE MIC: Spread a thin layer of vegan mayo (a couple tablespoons) over the parbaked crust and replace the cheese mix with 2¼ cups shredded vegan mozzarella. Use vegan pepperoni for the meat. (Vegan pepperoni tends to dry out a little in the oven, so drizzle some olive oil over it after the pizza comes out.) Finish with 2 to 3 tablespoons grated vegan parmesan.

WHAT WE DO

This pizza is like an exclamation point on how Down North comes from another angle. We don't do a basic meat lover's pizza. Instead, we season ground beef kinda like sausage, with toasted fennel, garlic, and onion, and we scatter that on the pie with our halal beef pepperoni. Then we throw on some pickled banana pepper rings and some blanched kale. Finally, the drizzle: our Honey Chipotle Sauce makes this pizza slam dancing. It's what we do. How we get it done.

1 teaspoon fennel seeds

6 ounces halal ground beef

1 teaspoon garlic powder

1 teaspoon onion powder

About ½ teaspoon kosher salt

About ¼ teaspoon freshly ground black pepper

1 to 2 large kale leaves (about 1 ounce), tough center stems cut out

¾ cup shredded low-moisture whole-milk mozzarella

¾ cup shredded provolone cheese

¾ cup shredded sharp white cheddar cheese

1 Down North Pizza Crust (page 30), parbaked in the pan

36 thin slices of beef pepperoni (about ½ cup)

⅓ cup chopped pickled banana pepper rings

¼ cup Honey Chipotle Sauce (page 43)

Preheat the oven: If you have a pizza oven, preheat it to 700°F. In a home oven, set the temperature to 500° or 550°F, with the convection setting on if you have it, and put a baking stone or baking steel on a top rack of the oven set 6 to 8 inches below the heat. Preheat the oven for 1 hour.

Make the beef sausage: Place the fennel seeds in a large dry skillet over medium heat and toast for 2 to 3 minutes, until they smell good (not burnt), shaking the pan a couple times. Add the ground beef and sprinkle on the garlic powder and onion powder. Break up the beef with a spoon or spatula, evenly mixing in the spices, and cook until the beef is browned, 5 to 6 minutes. Season with the salt and black pepper until it tastes good to you, then pour off the fat and juices and set the seasoned meat aside.

Blanch the kale: Fill a large bowl with ice cubes and water. Bring a large pot of water to a boil and drop in the kale leaves; cook until they turn bright green, about 30 seconds or so. Remove the kale with tongs or a slotted spoon and dunk it in the ice water to stop the cooking. Transfer the kale to a paper towel to drain; when it's kinda dry, roughly chop it and set aside.

Prep the pizza: In a medium bowl, mix the mozz, provolone, and cheddar cheeses. Spread the cheese mix evenly over the pizza crust in the pan, and make sure it's pushed all the way to the edges. You want a good amount of cheese touching the pan to create a crispy "fence" all around the edges. Cover the cheese layer with the beef pepperoni slices to make 6 rows of 6 slices each. Crumble on the beef sausage in the blank spaces alongside the pepperoni rows, then scatter on the chopped kale and the chopped pickled banana peppers.

Bake: Slide the pan onto the baking stone or steel and cook until the edges of the pizza are dark brown, 10 to 15 minutes. In a home oven, if the edges aren't looking dark brown after 10 minutes, switch on the broiler setting. (With electric ovens, you may have to open the oven door for 10 seconds to make sure the broiler turns on.) Continue cooking for a few minutes, until the pizza edges are dark brown but not burnt. Watch it like a hawk!

Slice and finish: Remove the pan from the oven and put it on a heatproof surface. Run a wide metal spatula around the edges of the pan to loosen the pizza, then use the spatula to pop out the pizza and move it to a cutting board. Let it cool for a minute, then slice into 6 pieces. Drizzle with the sauce in a bad-ass zigzag pattern and then have at it.

remix

VEGAN WHAT WE DO: Use vegan mayo in the Honey Chipotle Sauce. Spread a thin layer of vegan mayo (a couple tablespoons) over the parbaked crust and replace the cheese mix with 2¼ cups vegan mozzarella. Also replace the sausage and pepperoni with vegan sausage (see page 23) and vegan pepperoni (page 95). (Vegan pepperoni tends to dry out a little in the oven, so drizzle some olive oil over it after the pizza comes out of the oven.)

the game

You might want to make extra seasoned beef. It's so good, whether on fries, with nachos, or in tacos. Double the amounts here and you'll get about 3 cups total—¾ cup for the pizza, plus 2¼ cups to use on something else. The seasoned beef keeps for a few days, covered, in the fridge.

1981   The "Just Say No" to Drugs Campaign begins and D.A.R.E. (Drug Abuse Resistance Education) programs proliferate across the country. D.A.R.E. programs are instituted in public schools nationwide despite the lack of evidence of their positive impact on youth.[65]

The blue cheese crumble on this pie was an afterthought. We were looking through a different Philly pizza joint's Insta one day, and we saw that their buffalo chicken pizza looked just like ours. We need all our pies to have a signature look, so we added a little blue cheese crumble to garnish the top. That bit was never a taste thing; it's there to make this is a Down North pizza like nobody else's. To say, "Yeah, that's us."

¾ cup shredded low-moisture whole-milk mozzarella

¾ cup shredded provolone cheese

¾ cup shredded sharp white cheddar cheese

1 Down North Pizza Crust (page 30), parbaked in the pan

1¼ cups cubed Roasted Chicken Thighs (page 56)

¼ cup Norffalo Sauce (page 35)

¼ cup store-bought creamy blue cheese dressing

2 to 3 tablespoons crumbled Gorgonzola

Preheat the oven: If you have a pizza oven, preheat it to 700°F. In a home oven, set the temperature to 500° or 550°F, with the convection setting on if you have it, and put a baking stone or baking steel on a top rack of the oven set 6 to 8 inches below the heat. Preheat the oven for 1 hour.

Prep the pizza: In a medium bowl, mix the mozz, provolone, and cheddar cheeses. Spread the mix evenly over the pizza crust in the pan, and make sure it's pushed all the way to the edges. You want a good amount of cheese touching the pan to create a crispy "fence" all around the edges. Place the cubed chicken all over the top.

Bake: Slide the pan onto the baking stone or steel and cook until the edges of the pizza are dark brown, 10 to 15 minutes. In a home oven, if the edges aren't looking dark brown after 10 minutes, switch on the broiler setting. (With electric ovens, you may have to open the oven door for 10 seconds to make sure the broiler turns on.) Continue cooking for a few minutes, until the pizza edges are dark brown but not burnt. Watch it like a hawk!

Slice and finish: Remove the pan from the oven and put it on a heatproof surface. Run a wide metal spatula around the edges of the pan to loosen the pizza, then use the spatula to pop out the pizza and move it to a cutting board. Let it cool for a minute, then slice into 6 pieces. Drizzle with the Norffalo Sauce and the blue cheese dressing in zigzag stripes. Garnish with the crumbled blue cheese.

the game

We roast our chicken thighs in-house. For the pizza, you could substitute the same amount of rotisserie chicken. Just pull the cooked meat off the bone, remove the skin, and cube it. Add Montreal steak seasoning to taste.

1983 The U.S. Department of Justice awards the first contract ever to design, build, finance, and operate a correctional facility to the Corrections Corporation of America (CCA), marking the start of the U.S. private prison system.

THAT'S US

remix

VEGETARIAN YEAH THAT'S US: Replace the chicken with the same amount of vegetarian chicken (see page 22). Season it with the spices as it says for the Roasted Chicken Thighs recipe (page 56), but hold back on the salt if your vegetarian chicken is already seasoned. Cook according to the package directions, which probably means just heating it through.

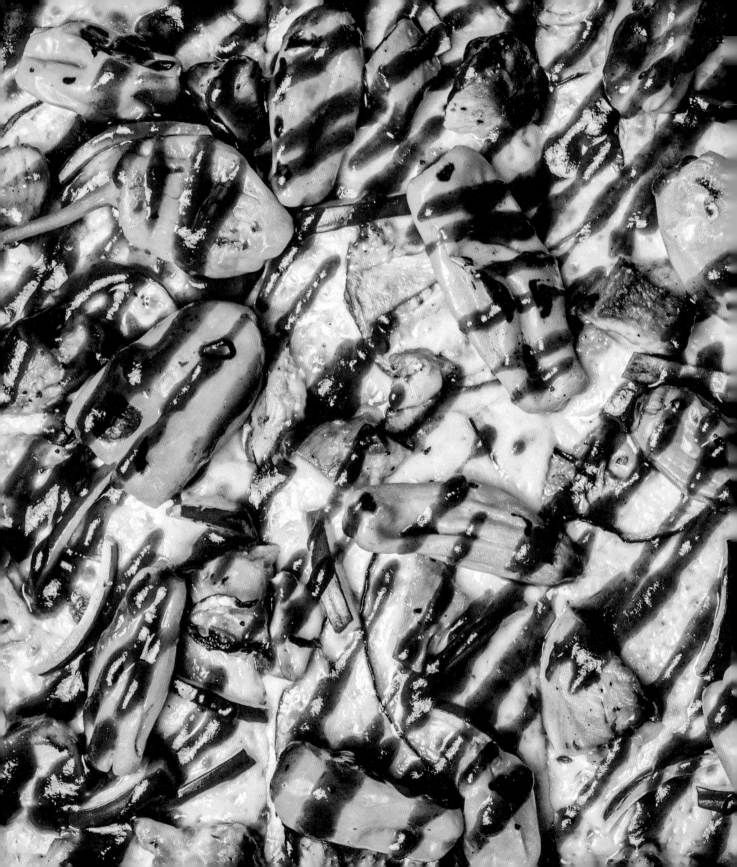

BIG HEAD

If you're from Philly, you know what Big Head means. Let's say a girl likes you. She might look you over and say, "Hey, Big Head, what you doin'?" It's one of them gritty Philly terms of endearment. In my hood, BBQ chicken was a classic pizza, so I'm gassin' up my hood with this pie. We step it up with a BBQ sauce I mix up with fresh ginger, molasses, and all kinds of spices. Plus, some pepperoncini on top of the BBQ chicken to balance the sweet with a little zing.

¾ cup shredded low-moisture whole-milk mozzarella

¾ cup shredded provolone cheese

¾ cup shredded sharp white cheddar cheese

1 Down North Pizza Crust (page 30), parbaked in the pan

2 cups cubed Roasted Chicken Thighs (page 56)

½ cup thin-sliced red onion strips

½ cup whole or sliced pepperoncini

⅓ cup Flip Side BBQ Sauce (page 39) or House BBQ Sauce (page 38)

Preheat the oven: If you have a pizza oven, preheat it to 700°F. In a home oven, set the temperature to 500° or 550°F, with the convection setting on if you have it, and put a baking stone or baking steel on a top rack of the oven set 6 to 8 inches below the heat. Preheat the oven for 1 hour.

Prep the pizza: In a medium bowl, mix the mozz, provolone, and cheddar cheeses. Spread the cheese mix evenly over the crust in the pan, and make sure it's pushed all the way to the edges. You want a good amount of cheese touching the pan to create a crispy "fence" all around the edges. Spread the cubed chicken, red onion strips, and pepperoncini slices over the cheese. You should barely see any cheese when you're done.

Bake: Slide the pan onto the baking stone or steel and cook until the edges of the pizza are dark brown, 10 to 15 minutes. In a home oven, if the edges aren't looking dark brown after 10 minutes, switch on the broiler setting. (With electric ovens, you may have to open the oven door for 10 seconds to make sure the broiler turns on.) Continue cooking for a few minutes, until the pizza edges are dark brown but not burnt. Watch it like a hawk!

Slice and finish: Remove the pan from the oven and put it on a heatproof surface. Run a wide metal spatula around the edges of the pan to loosen the pizza, then use the spatula to pop out the pizza and move it to a cutting board. Let it cool for a minute, then slice into 6 pieces. Drizzle the BBQ sauce in a bad-ass zigzag pattern over the top and dig in.

1984 The Comprehensive Crime Control Act of 1984 is signed into law. One of the 20th century's most significant pieces of crime legislation, it establishes mandatory minimum sentences for drug offenses, especially those involving small amounts of cannabis. This act and the 1986 Anti-Drug Abuse Act, which dictates much harsher sentences for possession of crack than for powder cocaine, establish a racialized and wide disparity between Black and white defendants.[66,67,68]

MAKES ONE 10-INCH
SQUARE PIE

BREAK YOU OFF

My guy Myles wanted to do a lamb sausage white pizza. We spiced up some ground lamb with jerk seasoning, and at first we were just gonna finish it with za'atar. Then I thought, *We got this roasted garlic honey that's been sittin' on the shelf*. After sittin' there for months, it got so pungent and garlicky that I figured it'd be dope drizzled on top. When we tasted it, we both looked at each other, like, "Oh, shit! We got it!" We put this pizza on the menu on a Thursday, and it was sold out by Saturday afternoon. It's been a Down North staple ever since. It's part of our roots. Go ahead. Break off a slice.

1 tablespoon Garlic Confit (see sidebar, page 47)

1 cup honey

8 ounces ground lamb

1 tablespoon dried jerk seasoning

1½ teaspoons ground fennel

1 teaspoon freshly ground black pepper

½ teaspoon kosher salt

¾ cup shredded low-moisture whole-milk mozzarella

¾ cup shredded provolone cheese

¾ cup shredded sharp white cheddar cheese

¼ cup whole-milk ricotta

1 Down North Pizza Crust (page 30), parbaked in the pan

2 generous teaspoons za'atar seasoning

Make the roasted garlic honey: In a small bowl, grab a fork and mash the garlic confit to a fine paste. You should have about 1 tablespoon. Tilt the bowl so the paste is on the side of the bowl, then mix in a little water, just a few drops at a time, until the paste is just slightly thinner. Add the honey and mix well. The garlic honey should be kinda thick and squirtable, a little thicker than sriracha sauce. Put the honey in a squirt bottle and keep it at room temperature. You can use it right away, but the longer it sits, the more pungent and garlicky it gets, which is how we like it at the shop.

Preheat the oven: If you have a pizza oven, preheat it to 700°F. In a home oven, set the temperature to 500° or 550°F, with the convection setting on if you have it, and put a baking stone or baking steel on a top rack of the oven set 6 to 8 inches below the heat. Preheat the oven for 1 hour.

Season the meat: In a medium bowl, mix the ground lamb, jerk seasoning, fennel, pepper, and salt, squeezing it in your hands to mix it good.

Prep the pizza: In a medium bowl, mix the mozz, provolone, and cheddar cheeses. Spread the ricotta over the pizza dough in the pan, then scatter on the cheese mix, pushing both toppings all the way to the edges. You want a good amount of cheese touching the pan to create a crispy "fence" all around the edges. Cover the cheese with crumbles of the lamb sausage until you can barely see the cheese underneath.

Bake: Slide the pan onto the baking stone or steel and cook until the edges of the pizza are dark brown and the lamb is cooked through (150°F on an instant-read thermometer), 10 to 15 minutes. In a home oven, if the edges aren't looking dark brown after 10 minutes, switch on the broiler setting. (With electric ovens, you may have to open the oven door for 10 seconds to make sure the broiler turns on.) Continue cooking for a few minutes, until the pizza edges are dark brown but not burnt. Watch it like a hawk!

Slice and finish: Remove the pan from the oven and put it on a heatproof surface. Run a wide metal spatula around the edges of the pan to loosen the pizza, then use the spatula to pop out the pizza and move it to a cutting board. Let it cool for a minute, then slice into 6 pieces. Drizzle about 2 tablespoons of that garlic honey on a diagonal across the pizza, then shower it from the sky with the za'atar.

1984 The Sentencing Reform Act is passed to reform sentencing practices and restrict judicial discretion through the creation of mandatory sentencing guidelines. The act also abolishes federal parole.[69,70,71]

I'M A BOSS

Here's another DN classic, our turkey lover's pizza with turkey sausage, turkey pepperoni, mushrooms, and peppers. We started making this one with our bodega sauce, a sweet and tangy combo of tamarind and Malta Goya that we got from the corner store. But people started asking for Norf Sauce instead. Give the people what they want. Let them call the shots. Just like Meek Mill, in "I'm a Boss."

¾ cup shredded low-moisture whole-milk mozzarella

¾ cup shredded provolone cheese

¾ cup shredded sharp white cheddar cheese

1 Down North Pizza Crust (page 30), parbaked in the pan

36 thin slices turkey pepperoni (about ⅔ cup)

½ cup crumbled turkey sausage (about 3 ounces)

½ cup Sautéed Mushrooms (page 55)

¼ cup julienned red bell pepper

¾ cup Norf Sauce (page 34)

2 heaping tablespoons grated grana padano or parmesan cheese

Preheat the oven: If you have a pizza oven, preheat it to 700°F. In a home oven, set the temperature to 500° or 550°F, with the convection setting on if you have it, and put a baking stone or baking steel on a top rack of the oven set 6 to 8 inches below the heat. Preheat the oven for 1 hour.

Prep the pizza: In a medium bowl, mix the mozz, provolone, and cheddar cheeses. Spread the cheese mix evenly over the crust in the pan, and make sure it's pushed all the way to the edges. You want a good amount of cheese touching the pan to create a crispy "fence" all around the edges. Lay the pepperoni slices over the cheese to make 6 rows of 6 slices each. Put the bits of sausage in the spaces between the rows, then scatter the mushrooms and red bell pepper evenly over the top.

Bake: Slide the pan onto the baking stone or steel and cook until the edges of the pizza are dark brown, 10 to 15 minutes. In a home oven, if the edges aren't looking dark brown after 10 minutes, switch on the broiler setting. (With electric ovens, you may have to open the oven door for 10 seconds to make sure the broiler turns on.) Continue cooking for a few minutes, until the pizza edges are dark brown but not burnt. Watch it like a hawk!

Slice and finish: Remove the pan from the oven and put it on a heatproof surface. Run a wide metal spatula around the edges of the pan to loosen the pizza, then use the spatula to pop out the pizza and move it to a cutting board. Let it cool for a minute, then slice into 6 pieces. Spoon big, wide (about 2 inches wide) diagonal stripes of Norf Sauce over the top and finish with the grated cheese.

MAY 13, 1985 The City of Philadelphia Police Department drops a C-4 bomb onto the home of members of MOVE, a grassroots organization that stood against racial and environmental injustice.[72]

remix

VEGAN I'M A BOSS: Spread a thin layer of vegan mayo (a couple tablespoons) over the parbaked crust and replace the cheese mix with 2¼ cups shredded vegan mozzarella. Swap out the turkey pepperoni and turkey sausage for vegan pepperoni and vegan Italian sausage (see page 23). (Vegan pepperoni tends to dry out a little in the oven, so drizzle some olive oil over it after the pizza comes out of the oven.) For the finish, use 2 to 3 tablespoons grated vegan parmesan.

FLIP SIDE

Peedi Crakk, the rapper on the song "Flipside," is Puerto Rican, and this is my take on island-style pizza. I caramelize some pineapple 'til it's drippin' with flavor. We don't do ham at Down North, so I use beef bacon here. And I knock the whole thing up with pickled jalapeños and BBQ sauce. Before you judge, try a slice. I had this Italian nonna come in and tell me, "Pineapple on pizza? That's blasphemy." I handed her a slice, and she couldn't believe how much she liked it. If you really want to make it next-level, use the Flip Side BBQ Sauce (page 39) instead of the House BBQ Sauce. The Flip Side's got flavor up the ying-yang.

4 or 5 strips of beef bacon (4 ounces)

4 tablespoons (½ stick) unsalted butter

1 cup chopped fresh or canned pineapple, in about 1-inch pieces

¼ cup sugar

Juice of ¼ lemon

¾ cup shredded low-moisture whole-milk mozzarella

¾ cup shredded provolone cheese

¾ cup shredded sharp white cheddar cheese

1 Down North Pizza Crust (page 30), parbaked in the pan

¼ cup Flip Side BBQ Sauce (page 39) or House BBQ Sauce (page 38)

About ⅓ cup chopped pickled jalapeños or sliced fresh jalapeños

Crisp the bacon: Preheat your oven to 350°F. Lay out the bacon in a small sheet pan and bake it up nice and crisp, 15 to 20 minutes. Transfer the bacon to paper towels to drain; pour the bacon fat into a medium skillet. When the bacon has cooled, coarsely chop it and set aside until you are ready to make the pizza.

Preheat the oven: If you have a pizza oven, preheat it to 700°F. In a home oven, set the temperature to 500° or 550°F, with the convection setting on if you have it, and put a baking stone or baking steel on a top rack of the oven set 6 to 8 inches below the heat. Preheat the oven for 1 hour.

Glaze the pineapple: About 30 minutes before the oven is ready, add the butter to the bacon fat in the skillet and melt it over medium heat. Add the pineapple, sugar, and lemon juice and cook until the sugar foams up and starts to caramelize to a light amber color, about 10 minutes. Stir it good while it's cooking so the pineapple gets a thick glaze on it. Remove the skillet from the heat and let the pineapple cool in the pan. Careful: The glaze will be hot like molten lava!

Prep the pizza: In a medium bowl, mix the mozz, provolone, and cheddar cheeses. Spread the cheese mix evenly over the crust in the pan, and make sure it's pushed all the way to the edges. You want a good amount of cheese touching the pan to create a crispy "fence" all around the edges. Distribute the bacon pieces evenly over the cheese. Spoon the gobs of glazed pineapple into the negative spaces around the bacon. If using fresh jalapeños, scatter them over the top. If using pickled jalapeños, save them for a garnish.

Bake: Slide the pan onto the baking stone or steel and cook until the edges of the pizza are dark brown, 10 to 15 minutes. In a home oven, if the edges aren't looking dark brown after 10 minutes, switch on the broiler setting. (With electric ovens, you may have to open the oven door for 10 seconds to make sure the broiler turns on.) Continue cooking for a few minutes, until the pizza edges are dark brown but not burnt. Watch it like a hawk!

Slice and finish: Remove the pan from the oven and put it on a heatproof surface. Run a wide metal spatula around the edges of the pan to loosen the pizza, then use the spatula to pop out the pizza and move it to a cutting board. Let it cool for a minute, then slice into 6 pieces. Drizzle the BBQ sauce in generous zigzags over the top, and finish with the chopped pickled jalapeños (if using).

remix
VEGAN FLIP SIDE: Use the House BBQ Sauce, vegan bacon, and vegan butter. Spread a thin layer of vegan mayo (a couple tablespoons) over the parbaked crust and replace the cheese mix with 2¼ cups shredded vegan mozzarella.

1986 The Anti-Drug Abuse Act is signed into law. A seminal piece of crime legislation, it dictates much harsher sentences for possession of crack cocaine compared to powder cocaine, based on the scientifically unjustifiable ratio of 100:1. Combined with mandatory minimum legislation, this act lays the groundwork for racial sentencing disparities, which disproportionately impact Black people.[73]

SAY YES

When I first met Muhammad, I showed up with a cooler of fresh ingredients from Philly's Reading Terminal Market: jerk turkey sausage from Giunta's, butternut squash and kale from OK Produce, and cheeses like ricotta from Downtown Cheese. Muhammad doesn't do pork, so I got jerk turkey. I roasted the squash with garlic oil and made a lemon honey to drizzle over the top. I really wanted him to say yes to me workin' at Down North. He dug the pizza. He said yes.

1 small butternut squash (about 1½ pounds), peeled (see The Game)

About 2 tablespoons garlic oil (see The Game) or olive oil

¼ teaspoon ground cinnamon

¼ teaspoon ground cumin

Kosher salt and freshly ground black pepper

1 to 2 large kale leaves (about 1 ounce), tough center stems cut out

¼ cup whole-milk ricotta

½ medium lemon

¾ cup shredded low-moisture whole-milk mozzarella

¾ cup shredded provolone cheese

¾ cup shredded sharp white cheddar cheese

Roast the squash: Preheat your oven to 500°F. Trim the top and bottom ends from the squash, then cut it in half lengthways. Use a teaspoon to scrape out the seeds and strings, and discard. Cut the squash crosswise into ¼-inch-thick half-rounds. Spread out the squash slices flat in a large sheet pan. Drizzle on the garlic oil, cinnamon, and cumin, then season with about ¼ teaspoon salt and ¼ teaspoon pepper. Rub the seasoning into the squash with your hands until evenly coated. Roast the squash until it's tender but not total mush, about 10 minutes. Remove and let cool. You should have about 2 cups of squash. Set aside until you are ready to make the pizza.

Preheat the oven: If you have a pizza oven, preheat it to 700°F. In a home oven, set the temperature to 500° or 550°F, with the convection setting on if you have it, and put a baking stone or baking steel on a top rack of the oven set 6 to 8 inches below the heat. Preheat the oven for 1 hour.

Blanch the kale: Fill a large bowl with ice cubes and water. Bring a large pot of water to a boil and drop in the kale leaves, cooking until bright green, about 30 seconds or so. Remove the kale with tongs or a slotted spoon and dunk them into the ice water to stop the cooking. Then remove and set the kale aside on a paper towel to drain. When the leaves are kinda dry, roughly chop them.

Whisk the ricotta: Put the ricotta in a small bowl and squeeze in a generous teaspoon of lemon juice (squeeze through your fingers to catch the seeds). Season with about ½ teaspoon salt and ¼ teaspoon pepper, and whisk until everything's blended. Set aside.

Combine the cheese: In a medium bowl, mix the mozz, provolone, and cheddar cheeses, and set aside.

Season the turkey: In a medium bowl, quickly mix the ground turkey and jerk seasoning. Squish it between your clean fingers to get the seasoning all through the meat. Set aside.

8 ounces ground turkey, preferably dark meat

1 tablespoon dried jerk seasoning, plus some for garnish

1 Down North Pizza Crust (page 30), parbaked in the pan

1½ tablespoons honey

the game

Use a vegetable peeler to peel the butternut squash—just be sure to get down to the orange flesh. If the skin is really hard, prick it with a fork in a few places, microwave it for a minute to soften the skin, then peel it.

Get a little more flavor in the roasted squash by using garlic oil instead of plain olive oil. Garlic oil is your reward for making the Garlic Confit (sidebar, page 47), my preferred method for making roasted garlic.

Prep the pizza: Spread the ricotta mix over the crust in the pan but not all the way to the edges. Scatter the cheese mix over the ricotta, and make sure it's pushed all the way to the edges, past the ricotta. You want a good amount of cheese touching the pan to create a crispy "fence" all around the edges.

Lay down about half the squash evenly over the cheese, leaving space between the pieces. (Snack on the remaining squash or puree it with some sour cream to make a roasted garlic dip for pita chips.) Put bits of the turkey sausage in the spaces around the squash until you can barely see the cheese, then top with the blanched kale.

Bake: Slide the pan onto the baking stone or steel and cook until the edges of the pizza are dark brown, 10 to 15 minutes. In a home oven, if the edges aren't looking dark brown after 10 minutes, switch on the broiler setting. (With electric ovens, you may have to open the oven door for 10 seconds to make sure the broiler turns on.) Continue cooking for a few minutes, until the pizza edges are dark brown but not burnt. Watch it like a hawk!

Prepare the lemon honey: While the pizza cooks, put the honey in a small bowl and squeeze in a generous teaspoon of lemon juice (again, through your fingers to catch seeds). Whisk until blended well; the consistency should be kinda medium-thin, like pure maple syrup. (If you started with a thick honey, drizzle in a little more lemon juice or water to get to that consistency.)

Slice and finish: Remove the pan from the oven and put it on a heatproof surface. Run a wide metal spatula around the edges of the pan to loosen the pizza, then use the spatula to pop out the pizza and move it to a cutting board. Let it cool for a minute, then slice into 6 pieces. Hit it with the lemon honey in a zigzag pattern across the top, sprinkle on some jerk seasoning, and dig in.

1989   Five young Black men are wrongfully convicted of varying crimes, including the attempted assault, rape, and murder of a white woman in Central Park, New York City. The group of young men is referred to as the Central Park Five in one of the most widely publicized criminal trials. All are exonerated in 2003 and one of the five, Yusef Salaam, goes on to serve as a New York City council member for the 9th district.[74,75]

MAKES ONE 10-INCH
SQUARE PIE

MY PART OF TOWN

the game

Ask your butcher to shave the sirloin for you. If that
doesn't fly, just toss your chunk of sirloin in the
freezer until it firms up but isn't frozen solid, 20 to
30 minutes. Then shave the sirloin yourself on a
mandoline. The mando's best here, but if you have
a knife that's sharp and thin like a sword—and have
ninja knife skills—you could do the job with that.

What's a Philly pizza shop without a cheesesteak pizza? A real beef, Cheez Whiz, and caramelized onion pie—all the flavors of a classic "whiz wit." In this town, if you're getting Whiz as your cheese, you order the cheesesteak "wit" onion or "wit-out." I'm always whiz wit 'cuz, for me, onions are what make a cheesesteak taste right. Here, I caramelize the onion and bump up my cheese sauce with onion powder to make it extra oniony. That steak-onion combo sends me right back to being a kid again in the late '80s, when "My Part of Town" was on the radio.

1 medium yellow onion

2 tablespoons canola oil

Pinch of kosher salt

8 ounces shaved beef sirloin (see The Game)

2 teaspoons Montreal steak seasoning

¾ cup shredded low-moisture whole-milk mozzarella

¾ cup shredded provolone cheese

¾ cup shredded sharp white cheddar cheese

1 Down North Pizza Crust (page 30), parbaked in the pan

About ⅓ cup Wiz Sauce (page 48), warmed

remix
LEHIGH VALLEY CHEESESTEAK PIZZA: Spoon about ¾ cup Norf Sauce (page 34) in thick diagonal stripes over the cooked pizza, then finish with a drizzle of the Wiz Sauce.

Preheat the oven: If you have a pizza oven, preheat it to 700°F. In a home oven, set the temperature to 500° or 550°F, with the convection setting on if you have it, and put a baking stone or baking steel on a top rack of the oven set 6 to 8 inches below the heat. Preheat the oven for 1 hour.

Caramelize the onion: Slice the onion hella thin (a mandoline works best). Heat 1 tablespoon of oil in a large skillet over medium-high heat. Add the onion and cook until it's translucent, 3 to 4 minutes, stirring occasionally. Stir in a pinch of salt, lower the heat to medium-low, and continue to cook until the onion is dark brown and caramelized, 20 to 30 minutes, tossing every few minutes. Turn off the heat and set aside. (If you see a brown film starting to form on the pan bottom, stir in a splash of water to deglaze it and mix it into the onion.)

Cook the steak: Heat the remaining tablespoon of oil in another large skillet over medium heat, and then add the shaved sirloin and steak seasoning. Toss and separate the pieces with tongs until the meat is cooked medium rare (still slightly pink), 4 to 5 minutes. Drain off and discard any juice and fat from the pan, then let the meat sit in the pan off the heat.

Prep the pizza: In a medium bowl, mix the mozz, provolone, and cheddar cheeses. Spread the cheese mix evenly over the crust in the pan, and make sure it's pushed all the way to the edges. You want a good amount of cheese touching the pan to create a crispy "fence" all around the edges. Cover with the steak and onion until you can barely see the cheese underneath.

Bake: Slide the pan onto the baking stone or steel and cook until the edges of the pizza are dark brown, 10 to 15 minutes. In a home oven, if the edges aren't looking dark brown after 10 minutes, switch on the broiler setting. (With electric ovens, you may have to open the oven door for 10 seconds to make sure the broiler turns on.) Continue cooking for a few minutes, until the pizza edges are dark brown but not burnt. Watch it like a hawk!

Slice and finish: Remove the pan from the oven and put it on a heatproof surface. Run a wide metal spatula around the edges of the pan to loosen the pizza, then use the spatula to pop out the pizza and move it to a cutting board. Let it cool for a minute, then slice into 6 pieces. Drizzle on that Wiz Sauce and grab a slice.

MAKES ONE 10-INCH
SQUARE PIE

TALES OF A HUSTLER

Smoking brisket is one of my favorite pastimes, and "Tales of a Hustler" is one of my favorite songs. It had to be a special pie that I would give this name to, and brisket pizza was the one. The smoky, juicy, black-as-night brisket, with the spicy Harissa Cheese Sauce and the sharp Pikliz Haitian pickles, goes hard. Like puttin' that song on repeat, I could eat this pizza over and over.

1 small brisket, flat or point, about 2 pounds, with silver skin and excess fat trimmed (if you don't have a smoker, see The Game)

2 tablespoons any mustard (yellow, brown, or Dijon)

2 teaspoons kosher salt

1 teaspoon freshly ground black pepper

½ teaspoon garlic powder

½ teaspoon onion powder

2 teaspoons berbere spice blend

1 cup apple cider vinegar

¼ cup fresh lime juice

¾ cup shredded low-moisture whole-milk mozzarella

¾ cup shredded provolone cheese

¾ cup shredded sharp white cheddar cheese

1 Down North Pizza Crust (page 30), parbaked in the pan

¼ cup Harissa Cheese Sauce (page 48)

½ cup Pikliz (page 52) or other spicy pickles

A few sprigs fresh thyme

Smoke the brisket: Fire up a smoker to 225° to 250°F. (If you don't have a smoker, see The Game.) Rub the mustard evenly all over the brisket—it'll help bind the seasonings to the meat and form a nice crust. Season the meat with the salt, pepper, garlic powder, onion powder, and 1 teaspoon of berbere spice blend.

Place the seasoned brisket in the smoker and smoke until the meat reaches an internal temperature of about 190°F (as measured on an instant-read thermometer). It'll seem like it takes forever—anywhere from 5 to 8 hours, depending on your meat and your smoker. The goal is to maintain a steady 250°F temperature in the smoker.

Spray the brisket and finish: Once you get the meat smoking, combine the vinegar, lime juice, and remaining teaspoon of berbere spice in a spray bottle. Shake it well, until the liquid changes color. Spray the brisket with this mixture every 30 to 40 minutes to help form a crunchy bark. (Settle in for the process. Good barbecue takes time.) About midway through the smoking (after 3 to 4 hours), wrap the brisket tightly in 2 layers of heavy-duty foil; you don't want any gaps or leaks. Starting around the 4-hour mark, take the temperature of the brisket every hour. When the brisket reaches 190°F (tested through the foil), take it off the smoker and put it on a cutting board (a grooved one is best, since it may leak a little). Let the brisket sit in the foil for at least 30 minutes or up to 1 hour. If you want to make the brisket further ahead, preheat a small cooler by filling it with hot water and closing the lid. After 15 minutes, dump the water and line the cooler with thick bath towels. Lay the foil-wrapped brisket on a tray to catch any drips then lay the tray in the bottom of the preheated cooler, and cover it with thick bath towels. Close the lid and the brisket will stay warm and juicy for up to 3 hours.

Preheat the oven: If you have a pizza oven, preheat it to 700°F. In a home oven, set the temperature to 500° or 550°F, with the convection setting on if you have it, and put a baking stone or baking steel on a top rack of the oven set 6 to 8 inches below the heat. Preheat the oven for 1 hour.

Slice the brisket: When the oven is hot, unwrap the brisket and slice it about ⅛ inch thick across the grain. (It's important to slice across the grain because it makes the meat easier to chew so it tastes more tender.)

Prep the pizza: In a medium bowl, mix the mozz, provolone, and cheddar cheeses. Spread the cheese mix evenly over the crust in the pan, and make sure it's pushed all the way to the edges. You want a good amount of cheese touching the pan to create a crispy "fence" all around the edges.

Cover the cheese with about 8 ounces of the brisket slices, until you can barely see the cheese underneath. (You'll have a little brisket left over. Eat it straight. Pile it on a sandwich. Douse it in Flip Side BBQ sauce, page 39. Do it up any which way!)

Bake: Slide the pan onto the baking stone or steel and cook until the edges of the pizza are dark brown, 10 to 15 minutes. In a home oven, if the edges aren't looking dark brown after 10 minutes, switch on the broiler setting. (With electric ovens, you may have to open the oven door for 10 seconds to make sure the broiler turns on.) Continue cooking for a few minutes, until the pizza edges are dark brown but not burnt. Watch it like a hawk!

Slice and finish: Remove the pan from the oven and put it on a heatproof surface. Run a wide metal spatula around the edges of the pan to loosen the pizza, then use the spatula to pop out the pizza and move it to a cutting board. Let it cool for a minute, then slice into 6 pieces. Drizzle on the cheese sauce, garnish with the Pikliz, and finish with a sprinkling of fresh thyme leaves.

the game

If you don't have a smoker, just buy some smoked and sliced brisket from your favorite BBQ joint. Skip the whole cooking process, but do sprinkle it with a teaspoon of berbere spice blend to get that flavor in there.

If you're not into the spicy cheese sauce, try this with Beer Cheese Sauce (page 48). I made that for a collab pizza with Philly's Triple Bottom Brewing, and it's dope. Triple Bottom also hires formerly incarcerated people, so we do lots of collabs with them.

1990s   This decade marks a period of socioeconomic progress and advancement for some Black people, yet it is also the era of zero tolerance and Black youth being vilified as "thugs" and "super predators." This punitive and racist logic turns the hallways of education into a pathway to prison, known as the "the school-to-prison pipeline." Metal detectors adorn school entryways and local police patrol hallways, adultifying Black youth and destroying the public's awareness of Black youth joy, need, pain, and trauma.[76,77,78,79]

MARCH 7, 1994   California's Three Strikes Law takes effect and two counts of petty theft with a prior carries consecutive sentences of twenty-five years to life in prison. Seventy-two percent of California voters endorse it, increasing the maximum sentence from under four years to an indeterminate life sentence with no possibility of parole for fifty years. This law fuels a nationwide trend of states passing zero-tolerance, mandatory-minimum laws, further expanding the carceral state and growth of mass incarceration.[80]

CROSS THE BORDER

MAKES ONE 10-INCH SQUARE PIE

#need justice knead dough

During our popups, before Down North opened, I put together this straight-up Taco Tuesday pie with the Old El Paso seasoning packet for that comfort food vibe. To step it up, I roasted poblano chiles and made cumin sour cream. With the seasoned beef and onion, crunchy lettuce, and chopped tomatoes over all that bubbly cheese, people popped out for this pizza.

1 pound ground beef

½ medium yellow onion, finely chopped (about ½ cup)

1 (1-ounce) packet Old El Paso taco seasoning

¾ cup water

2 fresh poblano chiles

½ cup sour cream

½ teaspoon ground cumin

¼ teaspoon kosher salt

¾ cup shredded low-moisture whole-milk mozzarella

¾ cup shredded provolone cheese

¾ cup shredded sharp white cheddar cheese

1 Down North Pizza Crust (page 30), parbaked in the pan

About 1½ cups shredded romaine lettuce

About ½ cup diced plum tomatoes

Preheat the oven: If you have a pizza oven, preheat it to 700°F. In a home oven, set the temperature to 500° or 550°F, with the convection setting on if you have it, and put a baking stone or baking steel on a top rack of the oven set 6 to 8 inches below the heat. Preheat the oven for 1 hour.

Prepare the meat: Cook the beef in a medium skillet on medium heat until it browns, about 5 minutes, breaking it up with a spoon or spatula as it cooks. Add the onion and cook until it softens, another 3 or 4 minutes. Stir in the taco seasoning and the water. Reduce the heat to medium-low and simmer until the liquid thickens and coats the meat, 3 to 4 minutes. Set aside.

Roast the poblano: Using tongs, hold the poblano chiles over a medium-high gas flame, or put on a hot grill or under a broiler, until they're blackened and blistered all over, about 10 minutes, turning them for even blackening. When charred all over, place the chiles in a small container and cover with plastic wrap. Let steam for 15 minutes. When cool enough to handle, peel off and discard the skins. Slit the chiles lengthwise and pull out and discard the stem, ribs, and seeds. Slice the pieces of roasted poblano lengthwise into thin strips.

Prepare the sauce: In a cup or small bowl, whisk together the sour cream, cumin, and salt. Pour it into a small squirt bottle and chill until ready to use.

Prep the pizza: In a medium bowl, mix the mozz, provolone, and cheddar cheeses. Spread the cheese mix evenly over the crust in the pan, and make sure it's pushed all the way to the edges. You want a good amount of cheese touching the pan to create a crispy "fence" all around the edges. Cover with the seasoned beef until you can barely see the cheese underneath.

Bake: Slide the pan onto the baking stone or steel and cook until the edges of the pizza are dark brown, 10 to 15 minutes. In a home oven, if the edges aren't looking dark brown after 10 minutes, switch on the broiler setting. (With electric ovens, you may have to open the oven door for 10 seconds to make sure the broiler turns on.) Continue cooking for a few minutes, until the pizza edges are dark brown but not burnt. Watch it like a hawk!

Slice and finish: Remove the pan from the oven and put it on a heatproof surface. Run a wide metal spatula around the edges of the pan to loosen the pizza, then use the spatula to pop out the pizza and move it to a cutting board. Let it cool for a minute, then slice into 6 pieces. Top with the shredded lettuce, diced tomatoes, and the poblano strips. Squirt the cumin sour cream in diagonal stripes over the whole pie, then grab a slice.

SEPTEMBER 1994   President Bill Clinton signs into law the Violent Crime Control and Law Enforcement Act, a vast catchall tough-on-crime bill. Criminal justice experts say this law helps lay the groundwork for mass incarceration that devastates America's Black communities.[81,82] This Act also bars incarcerated students from accessing Pell Grant funds to participate in and graduate from college programs.[83]

A LONG WALK

This one's my ode to Jill Scott, Philadelphia's soulful songstress. The lyrics for "A Long Walk" are all about being in love with someone and getting to know each other. Here, I was leaning toward pizza being a comfort food and this easygoing pie being a good way for people to get to know me. Who doesn't like the taste of creamy pesto chicken and roasted peppers? You put that on a fluffy, crusty pizza with all that melty cheese? Nothin' not to love about it.

¾ cup shredded low-moisture whole-milk mozzarella

¾ cup shredded provolone cheese

¾ cup shredded sharp white cheddar cheese

⅓ Basil-Pesto Cream Sauce (page 44), plus more as needed

1 Down North Pizza Crust (page 30), parbaked in the pan

About 1½ cups cubed Roasted Chicken Thighs (page 56)

½ cup sliced fire-roasted red bell pepper (in strips)

Preheat the oven: If you have a pizza oven, preheat it to 700°F. In a regular home oven, set the temperature to 500° or 550°F, with the convection setting on if you have it, and put a baking stone or baking steel on a top rack of the oven rack set 6 to 8 inches below the heat. Preheat the oven for 1 hour.

Prep the pizza: In a medium bowl, mix the mozz, provolone, and cheddar cheeses. Spread ⅓ cup of the pesto cream sauce over the crust in the pan, then spread the cheese mix evenly over the pesto. Make sure the cheese is pushed all the way to the edges. You want a good amount of cheese touching the pan to create a crispy "fence" all around the edges. Cover with the cubed chicken and roasted pepper.

Bake: Slide the pan onto the baking stone or steel and cook until the edges of the pizza are dark brown, 10 to 15 minutes. In a home oven, if the edges aren't looking dark brown after 10 minutes, switch on the broiler setting. (With electric ovens, you may have to open the oven door for 10 seconds to make sure the broiler turns on.) Continue cooking for a few minutes, until the pizza edges are dark brown but not burnt. Watch it like a hawk!

Slice and finish: Remove the pan from the oven and put it on a heatproof surface. Run a wide metal spatula around the edges of the pan to loosen the pizza, then use the spatula to pop out the pizza and move it to a cutting board. Let it cool for a minute, then slice into 6 pieces. Finish with a drizzle of pesto cream sauce.

2000s During the 2000s, the carceral state becomes increasingly bloated through racial profiling, "stop and frisk" policies, disproportionate minority contact in youth facilities, and felony disenfranchisement.[84],[85],[86],[87] The impact of these policies becomes increasingly more visible and felt beyond the Black community.

MAKES ONE 10-INCH
SQUARE PIE

SAUCE IT UP

I cooked this spicy Thai red curry chicken pizza on First We Feast's *Pizza Wars* show with Sean Evans and Nicole Russell. Sean is the host of the popular *Hot Ones* chile-eating show, and I figured this one would go over well with him. Warning: It's super spicy, especially if you make it with the hot sauce (see The Game). I don't call it "Sauce It Up" for nothin'!

About 2 cups Thai (red bird's-eye) chiles, stemmed and sliced crosswise into thin wheels (wear gloves!)

1 (1-inch) piece fresh ginger, peeled and thinly sliced

1 cup distilled white vinegar

1 cup water

5 tablespoons sugar

2 tablespoons kosher salt

¾ cup shredded low-moisture whole-milk mozzarella

¾ cup shredded provolone cheese

¾ cup shredded sharp white cheddar cheese

1 Down North Pizza Crust (page 30), parbaked in the pan

About 1½ cups cubed Spicy Pickle-Brined Roasted Chicken Thighs (page 57)

About ⅓ cup Quick Thai Red Curry Sauce (page 40), warmed

Chopped fresh cilantro, for garnish

Make the spicy pickles: Place the chiles and ginger in a pint glass mason jar with a lid. Combine the vinegar with the water, sugar, and salt in a small saucepan. Bring to a gentle simmer over medium-high heat, stirring just until the sugar and salt dissolve, then pour the hot pickling liquid over the chiles and ginger, filling the jar almost to the top. Screw on the lid and let stand at room temperature for at least 8 hours. (Or refrigerate for up to 6 months.)

Preheat the oven: If you have a pizza oven, preheat it to 700°F. In a home oven, set the temperature to 500° or 550°F, with the convection setting on if you have it, and put a baking stone or baking steel on a top rack of the oven set 6 to 8 inches below the heat. Preheat the oven for 1 hour.

Prep the pizza: In a medium bowl, mix the mozz, provolone, and cheddar cheeses. Spread the cheese mix evenly over the crust in the pan, and make sure it's pushed all the way to the edges. You want a good amount of cheese touching the pan to create a crispy "fence" all around the edges. Cover with the cubed chicken.

Bake: Slide the pan onto the baking stone or steel and cook until the edges of the pizza are dark brown, 10 to 15 minutes. In a home oven, if the edges aren't looking dark brown after 10 minutes, switch on the broiler setting. (With electric ovens, you may have to open the oven door for 10 seconds to make sure the broiler turns on.) Continue cooking for a few minutes, until the pizza edges are dark brown but not burnt. Watch it like a hawk!

Slice and finish: Remove the pan from the oven and put it on a heatproof surface. Run a wide metal spatula around the edges of the pan to loosen the pizza, then use the spatula to pop out the pizza and move it to a cutting board. Let it cool for a minute, then slice into 6 pieces. Finish with a drizzle of the curry sauce, some pickled Thai chiles, and chopped cilantro.

the game

If you want this pizza to be blow-your-head-off spicy, blend up a quick hot sauce for an extra drizzle. Before you build the pizza, scoop out and set aside half the pickled chiles for your garnish, and puree the rest of the pickle mix (chiles, ginger, and liquid) in a blender until smooth. Pour that hot sauce into a small squirt bottle and drizzle it in a bad-ass zigzag all over the curry sauce. Chile heads will love it!

To save time, you could just buy some spicy pickled peppers instead of making them from scratch.

2001 Studies show that one in every three Black boys born in 2001 could expect to go to prison in his lifetime, as could one in every six Latinos—compared to one in every seventeen white boys.[88]

125

MAKES ONE
10-INCH
SQUARE PIE

CHOPPED PIZZA

A few years ago, a producer from the *Chopped* TV show called me and asked me on the show. Guess where I prepped the food? In a hotel in Queens! I wanted to braise some spicy chicken for this one, and I love coconut milk. Add some garlic and ginger, a few spices like warm and tingly berbere seasoning, and it's the perfect braising liquid for chicken thighs. With that sauce boiled down so it can be drizzled, and a lime-cilantro garnish, this coconut braised chicken pizza slaps. My only regret on *Chopped* was they shoulda saved me for the last round. I woulda loved to win that $10 grand!

2 to 3 tablespoons canola oil

2 pounds boneless, skinless chicken thighs (about 8 thighs)

½ small red onion, finely chopped (about ½ cup)

3 medium garlic cloves, minced

1 (1½-inch) piece fresh ginger, peeled and minced (about 1 tablespoon)

1 tablespoon berbere spice blend

½ teaspoon ground cumin

½ teaspoon ground cinnamon

Preheat the oven: If you have a pizza oven, preheat it to 700°F. In a home oven, set the temperature to 500° or 550°F, with the convection setting on if you have it, and put a baking stone or baking steel on a top rack of the oven set 6 to 8 inches below the heat. Preheat the oven for 1 hour.

Cook the chicken thighs: Heat a Dutch oven over medium-hot heat. When hot, pour in enough oil to cover the bottom. Add the chicken thighs and sear until nicely browned all over, about 5 minutes per side. Remove the chicken to a cutting board and let cool.

Meanwhile, add the onion to the remaining oil in the pan and cook over medium heat for a couple minutes. Add the garlic, ginger, berbere spice, cumin, cinnamon, and red pepper flakes and let simmer for a few minutes, stirring now and then. Add the tomatoes and coconut milk, and bring to a simmer.

Dice the chicken and return it to the pan, then let everything simmer on medium-low heat until the flavors blend and the liquid reduces in volume a bit, 25 to 30 minutes. Taste and season with salt and black pepper until it seems good to you.

1 teaspoon red pepper
flakes

1 (14-ounce) can diced
tomatoes with juice

1 (14-ounce) can full-fat
coconut milk

Kosher salt and freshly
ground black pepper

¾ cup shredded low-
moisture whole-milk
mozzarella

¾ cup shredded provolone
cheese

¾ cup shredded sharp
white cheddar cheese

1 Down North Pizza Crust
(page 30), parbaked in
the pan

1 tablespoon chopped fresh
cilantro

1 lime, cut into wedges

Prep the pizza: In a medium bowl, mix the mozz, provolone, and cheddar cheeses. Spread the cheese mix evenly over the crust in the pan, and make sure it's pushed all the way to the edges. You want a good amount of cheese touching the pan to create a crispy "fence" all around the edges. Cover with the diced chicken so you can barely see the cheese.

Bake: Slide the pan onto the baking stone or steel and cook until the edges of the pizza are dark brown, 10 to 15 minutes. In a home oven, if the edges aren't looking dark brown after 10 minutes, switch on the broiler setting. (With electric ovens, you may have to open the oven door for 10 seconds to make sure the broiler turns on.) Continue cooking for a few minutes, until the pizza edges are dark brown but not burnt. Watch it like a hawk!

Slice and finish: Remove the pan from the oven and put it on a heatproof surface. Run a wide metal spatula around the edges of the pan to loosen the pizza, then use the spatula to pop out the pizza and move it to a cutting board. Let it cool for a minute, then slice into 6 pieces. Spoon the pan sauce over the top of the pizza in a diagonal zigzag pattern and garnish with the cilantro. Serve with the lime wedges, so err'body can squeeze a little over their slice.

OCTOBER 6, 2001 Congress passes the Patriot Act in the wake of terrorist attacks at the World Trade Center in New York City, the Pentagon, and Shanksville, Pennsylvania, on September 11, 2011. The Patriot Act ushers in a new era of state surveillance, profiling, and investigation at all levels of government that contradicts the civil liberties and civil rights of people, particularly for Muslim, religious, and political communities.[89,90]

GLAMOROUS LIFE

MAKES ONE 10-INCH
SQUARE PIE

There's nothing that signifies glamour more than seafood. There are a few steps here to make the sauces and fry the butterflied shrimp, but it's so worth it. Lump crab meat goes underneath the cheese in this one to keep the crab from burnin' up in the oven, and the fried shrimp is the crowning touch. A layer of Garlic-Parm Sauce gives it some creaminess, but I wanted another sauce, a red one, for the top. Something like vodka sauce, but not quite: more like Not Vodka Sauce. Add some fried kale—a little greenery for the scenery—and this pie makes you feel like you're on top of the world.

2 large kale leaves (about 1 ounce), tough center stems cut out (see The Game)

Vegetable oil, for frying

1 cup seafood fry mix, such as McCormick Golden Dipt Seafood Fry Mix

6 jumbo shrimp (21-25/pound, 4 to 6 ounces total), peeled, deveined, and butterflied, tail left on

¾ cup shredded low-moisture whole-milk fat mozzarella

¾ cup shredded provolone cheese

Preheat the oven: If you have a pizza oven, preheat it to 700°F. In a home oven, set the temperature to 500° or 550°F, with the convection setting on if you have it, and put a baking stone or baking steel on a top rack of the oven set 6 to 8 inches below the heat. Preheat the oven for 1 hour.

Prepare the kale: Fill a large bowl with ice cubes and water. Bring a large pot of water to a boil and drop in the kale leaves, cooking until they're bright green, about 30 seconds or so. Remove the leaves with tongs or a slotted spoon and dunk them in the ice water to stop the cooking. Then remove and set the kale on a paper towel to drain. Pat completely dry, then roughly chop the leaves. Press some paper toweling on it again to make sure it's dry.

Heat about 3 cups vegetable oil to about 350°F in a medium pot over medium heat (see The Game). When the oil is just right, drop in all the kale and fry until crisp, about 1 minute. Remove and drain on paper towels or a flat paper bag. Keep the oil at 350°F.

Fry the shrimp: Put the seafood fry mix in a medium bowl. Pour a few tablespoons of vegetable oil into another small bowl. Holding each shrimp by the tail one at a time, dip it into the oil to coat, then in the batter mix until thoroughly coated. Drop the shrimp into the 350°F frying oil, and fry until golden brown all over, about 3 minutes. Transfer to paper towels or a flat paper bag to drain. Set aside.

¾ cup shredded sharp white cheddar cheese

⅓ cup Garlic-Parm Sauce (page 46)

1 Down North Pizza Crust (page 30), parbaked in the pan

6 ounces lump crab meat

About ¼ cup Not Vodka Sauce (page 34)

Prep the pizza: In a medium bowl, mix the mozz, provolone, and cheddar cheeses. Spread the Garlic-Parm Sauce over the crust in the pan all the way to the edges. Scatter the crab evenly over the sauce. Then spread the cheese mix evenly over the crab, making sure the cheese is pushed all the way to the edges. You want a good amount of cheese touching the pan to create a crispy "fence" all around the edges.

Bake: Slide the pan onto the baking stone or steel and cook until the edges of the pizza are dark brown, 10 to 15 minutes. In a home oven, if the edges aren't looking dark brown after 10 minutes, switch on the broiler setting. (With electric ovens, you may have to open the oven door for 10 seconds to make sure the broiler turns on.) Continue cooking for a few minutes, until the pizza edges are dark brown but not burnt. Watch it like a hawk!

Slice and finish: Remove the pan from the oven and put it on a heatproof surface. Run a wide metal spatula around the edges of the pan to loosen the pizza, then use the spatula to pop out the pizza and move it to a cutting board. Let it cool for a minute, then slice into 6 pieces. Place a fried shrimp on each slice and then drizzle with the Not Vodka Sauce in a diagonal zigzag pattern. Garnish with the crispy kale and serve 'em up.

the game

If you want to skip deep-frying the kale, just use about 1 cup store-bought kale chips for the garnish.

Instead of deep-frying the shrimp, you can shallow-fry the breaded shrimp in a deep heavy skillet, such as cast-iron, in about ½ inch of 350°F oil until golden brown all over, about 3 minutes.

If you don't have a cooking thermometer, you can tell if the oil is hot enough for deep-frying by dropping a small piece of dry kale into the hot oil. It should start bubbling right away. If it just bubbles lazily, let the oil get a little hotter. If it bubbles wildly and splatters, lower the heat a bit.

JANUARY 2002 The Urban Institute publishes a report that describes the millions of dollars diverted away from community investment and into the literal incarceration of people from the same street block into prison and jails: "more than one million dollars are spent to incarcerate and return residents from [a] block in a single year."[91,92,93] This systemic cycle would lay the foundation for intergenerational incarceration and mass supervision within communities.[94,95]

2006 Six Black male high school students from Jena, Louisiana, are arrested for the attempted murder of a white male at the high school. The arrest happens in the midst of heightened racial tension at the school, where arson and nooses hanging from a tree plague the school environment. The "Jena Six" becomes a powerful reminder of the disproportionate, biased treatment of Black people that attempts to push them further into the criminal legal system.[96]

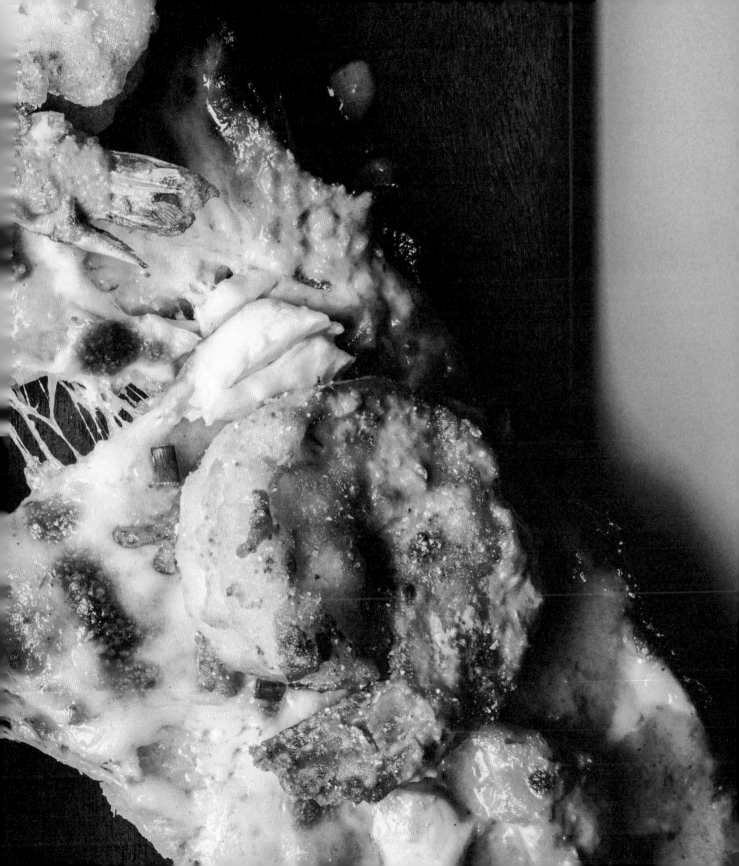

WHAT YA LIFE LIKE

WARNING: DO NOT TRY THIS AT HOME. Why would you? You don't have to. You can make pizza with dough. You can bake it in an oven, not a quasi sous vide machine made possible with an extension cord, a bucket, nail clippers, and an electrical outlet. (AGAIN: DO NOT TRY THIS AT HOME!) This recipe was born under the restrictions of a jailhouse. This is how I made pizza in prison. You can't get flour there, so it starts with ramen and Cheez-It crackers. Cash is illegal, too, but ramen is so common, it's a form of currency. (Vox did a whole video-story on it.) There's even a cookbook called *Prison Ramen*, and it's one of the most banned books in America.

I crushed the ramen noodles with Cheez-It crackers, mixed the dust with water to make a pizza dough, and grabbed whatever cheese, sauce, and toppings I could from the commissary, then I built the pizza and cooked it, all in my jail cell stinger (boiling water bath). Prison forces you to get creative like that.

```
3 (3-ounce) packages ramen noodles
½ (1-ounce) bag Cheez-It crackers (saltines work, too)
1 empty, sturdy large potato chip or tortilla chip bag
Squeeze cheese, such as Cheez Whiz
BBQ sauce
Salsa
Block cheese, such as provolone or cheddar
Spicy beef summer sausage
Kippered beef steak
Green and white crayons (optional)
```

Make the crust: Bust up the ramen and Cheez-Its as fine as you can. You're tryin' to make flour. (We used to throw the bags against the wall.) When they're crushed to dust, pour the ramen and Cheez-It dust into a big, empty chip bag. Add enough water to make a stiff dough, squeezing the bag down to the ingredients and smushing it around until everything is kinda soft, like stiff Play-Doh. Unchoke the bag and flatten it out, then flatten out the dough inside. You want the dough shaped flat, like a thin pizza crust. Tape shut the open end of the bag. (Tip: I used the little piece of tape from my deodorant lid.) Put the dough bag under your mattress or under two big-ass books, and let it sit there until it's stiff, maybe 20 minutes.

Prep the crust: Now you need a knife. You can't have a knife in prison, and if I did have one, I couldn't tell you I had one. So, you know those shaving mirrors you can put in a travel kit? Crack one in half and that's your knife. Take the knife and slice down the back seam of the chip bag. Make a good, clean cut to open up the bag and expose the pizza crust. With the bag open and the crust on a flat surface, squirt some squeeze cheese all over the dough, then spread it out with a plastic spoon. (The cheese acts like a sealant so the dough doesn't get soggy. Make sure you got complete coverage.)

Mix equal parts BBQ sauce and salsa to make about ½ cup total, then spread that over the cheese. (Jailhouse tomato sauce is gross; don't even think about using it.)

Prep the toppings: Now, cut down your cheese blocks. I used provolone, cheddar, or whatever I could get from the commissary. Those cheese blocks are full of preservatives, so they don't need refrigeration. Use your mirror knife (carefully; that shit will cut you) and shave the cheese into as thin slices as possible. You want maybe 1 cup or just shy of that. Scatter it over the sauce.

Now, you're gonna crisp up that summer sausage. Unwrap it, then put two pencils into each end of the sausage. That's your meat on a spit. To make a fire, grab a roll of toilet paper and roll it around your wrist in a spiral, maybe five times, to make a cone. Fires ain't allowed in jail cells, so we keep it hidden by using the toilet to suck down the smoke. Set your paper cone on the edge of the toilet and hold your spitted meat near the paper cone. Light the cone with a lighter, then flush the toilet. Roll the spitted meat in front of the fire and flush the toilet constantly to suck down the smoke and smell. Keep that up until the summer sausage is cooked even and crispy all over, 5 to 10 minutes. Yeah, you might need to make another paper cone if you didn't make it good enough the first time. (Ever wonder why inmates keep their jail cells immaculately clean? 'Cuz we have to cook, eat, and go to the bathroom in the same place!)

Now chop up your crispy summer sausage, and while you're at it, slice down your kippered beef steaks and cut them into squares. Cover the cheese with the chopped kippered steak and summer sausage. If you want the illusion of veg on there, shave some green crayon (peppers) and white crayon (onions) over the top. Your layers should be: dough, cheese sealant, sauce, cheese, meat, and optional "veg." Your pizza is all topped.

"Bake" the pizza: Fold the chip bag back over everything so the pizza is enclosed, and put it on a piece of cardboard or something sturdy so you can handle it easily. Slide the whole thing with the cardboard into a trash bag or another bigger bag. (We used thick, clear, plastic bags.) Position the pizza and cardboard so they're on the bottom of the bag with the pizza face up. You need to make this bag waterproof, so choke the plastic down over the pizza and tie it tight with a knot right over the middle of the pizza.

To cook the pizza, you drop this bag into a makeshift sous vide machine or boiling water bath—a.k.a., "stinger." To make it, you need an extension cord, a bucket, nail clippers, and your wall outlet. DO NOT TRY THIS AT HOME. Hell, you may not even want to try it in jail. If you blow the power, you blow it for the whole block. Not a good way to make friends.

Here's my stinger method: Separate the pieces of the nail clipper by taking out the metal pin from the cutter end. Bust open the female end of the extension cord, exposing the wires. Connect each of the two wires to the two holes in the clipper where the pin was, wrapping the wire in and around each hole. Take a soda cap or eraser as a ground and wedge it between the two metal sides of the clippers on the cutting end where the pin was. This ground is important because if those two metal sides touch, the two wires touch, and you blow the power. Now, take a rubber band or a ripped-up sheet and wrap it around the two pieces of metal with the ground wedged in between. You want that rubber band or sheet tight so your stinger setup doesn't fall apart, but not so tight that the metal sides touch.

Now, take a bucket, like a wash bucket, and line it with a trash bag. Fill it with water (a few quarts) and baking soda (about a tablespoon). (You can use salt, but baking soda is better so it doesn't oxidize your clippers.) Stick your clipper end of the extension cord into the water bucket. Plug the other end into the wall. You'll have boiling water in 10 minutes.

Lay the pizza setup on the boiling water. The cardboard holds it flat and keeps it floating. Lay a towel over the bucket and pizza setup to hold the heat in. Let it rock out until the cheese melts as good as it can (mozzarella melts better, and if you work in the prison kitchen, you might be able to get it). The pizza's done when the cheese melts and the ramen–Cheez-It crust gets firm and dry inside. It'll take about 30 minutes.

Unplug your stinger. Pull out your pizza. Cut it grandma style, and grab a slice.

PIZZA
COLLABS

A lot of magic happens at Down North. Celebrities like Al Roker have stopped by, grabbed a slice, and witnessed our mission in action. We also go around the country, collaborating with chefs and various other organizations.

These collabs started with a local series called "A Match Made in Philly." First up was chef Marc Vetri, chef of Vetri Cucina, with his Beef Shank Ragù, Smoked Scamorza, and Horseradish Pizza (page 144). The people dug it. Zahav's Mike Solomonov made another flavor bomb, Harissa Chicken Schnitzel Pizza (page 148). Other well-known Philly chefs, like Cristina Martinez, Randy Rucker, and Chad Williams also got involved, sharing their culinary skill. They came to the shop in North Philly, cooked with our chefs, mingled with the community, and learned what life is like in our part of the city.

Since then, we've done collabs around the country with luminaries like Marcus Samuelsson, who knocked out a berbere-spiked Doro Wat Pizza (page 155), and Reem Assil, who created a bangin' Pali Cali Pizza (page 158) with sumac and pomegranate molasses. (See page 209 for more info on all the chefs featured in this chapter.) All the chefs have been grateful for the experience. We have, too! It's not every day you can bring together different communities to cook side by side, share stories, and bridge divides between people who don't normally cross paths. This is the future direction of Down North. We're going to keep making our mind-blowing pizza, and we're going to keep spreading the word about reducing recidivism rates around the country. The power is in the people. —MUHAMMAD ABDUL-HADI

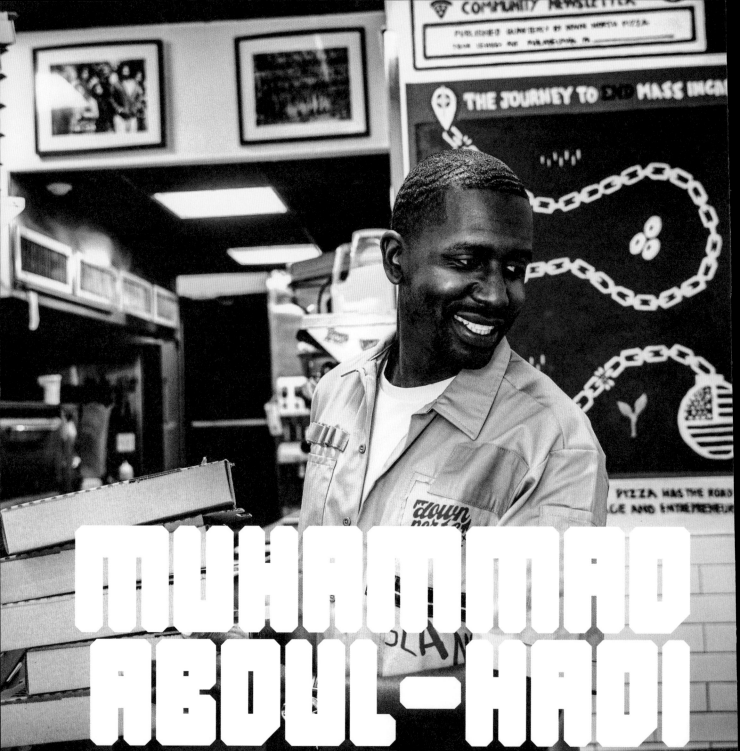

MUHAMMAD ABDUL-HADI

FOUNDER AND OWNER, DOWN NORTH

My father taught me one of the most important lessons: hope is an action, not a feeling.

To this day, brothers from all over Philadelphia tell me how grateful they are for the work of my father, Khalil Abdul-Hadi. He was a mechanical engineer who worked and traveled a lot, but when he was home, my father was deeply involved in strengthening our local community. He helped build religious centers around the city and went into places like the notorious Holmesburg Prison to steer brothers away from going back to gang life on the streets. Some of those guys ended up having their records expunged and became lawyers and accountants for the federal government. That's impactful change.

HELPING PEOPLE GET CLEAN

It left a big impression on me— bigger than I realized at the time. In my early twenties, I was headed down my own troubling path, committing nefarious acts, entering the street economy. My dad saw me going through life with no direction, searching for a purpose. He became a positive influence, but a few years later, in 2011, he passed away from prostate cancer. That really turned me around. I wish I had more time with him, and I got serious about building my own career. I wanted to help people in the community like he did, but on my own terms.

My first break was an entry-level position as House Manager at Gaudenzia, the biggest nonprofit addiction-treatment center in Pennsylvania. My job was to make sure people stuck with the program to get clean. I was a glorified babysitter, but it was gratifying work. Clients improved when they stayed in treatment instead of reverting to the streets. Over the next few years, I had jobs at various treatment centers, working my way up from Housing Manager to Supervisor to Director. When my mentor, Henry Bennett, started his own treatment center, Footprints to Recovery, he hired me to build out the entire housing program from scratch. I took to that job like a bird to the sky. That's when I realized I work better when I'm building something from nothing. After a couple years, Henry's investor partners bought him out, and he left the company. The investors brought in a new guy to increase our client base. Within a few months, the company went from just breaking even to grossing a couple million dollars a month. Part of that result was me making sure our clients stuck with the program. With all the success, both the new guy and I asked for equity in the company.

The investors shot it down, so the new guy and his business partner started their own addiction-recovery center, Liberation Way. They wanted me to come with them. The quality of the clinical treatment at Footprints was starting to go down, so I decided to leave. This time, though, I would start my own housing company so I could run my own business. Liberation Way opened in 2015 and hired my company, Legacy House, to handle housing services. I provided safe and stable housing, transportation, and other kinds of support to help our clients recover from addiction. We took them food shopping, to doctor's appointments . . . whatever they needed to stay in treatment. It worked: my clients got better. I was seeing real improvement in their personal lives and in their careers.

Some of my clients had valuable skills. They were electricians, plumbers, and carpenters. But they didn't want to go back to the trade unions. Historically speaking, Black folks don't fare too well in Philly's trade unions. At the time, I also wanted to get deeper into real estate. I was thinking back to those blueprints my dad was always working on as a mechanical engineer. As a kid, I dreamt of owning those buildings someday. Now, as an adult, I thought: *Maybe I could develop real estate to provide jobs for my recovery clients. I could hire them to renovate buildings in neglected neighborhoods and we'd turn crumbling eyesores into useful properties for the community.* That's when I bought the building at 28th and Lehigh in North Philly that eventually became Down North Pizza.

PIZZA PI

The Down North property sits right next to the local library in North Philly's Strawberry Mansion neighborhood. At first, I was going to make it a math tutoring center and hire formerly incarcerated folks to run it. I was going to call it Pizza Pi: give kids free pizza to get them in the door, keep them off the streets, and get them working on their math skills. We'd serve that gooey, cheesy square pizza like you get on Fridays at school. Comfort food they'd love. But the tutoring center was a heavier lift than I expected. When you're dealing with kids, regulations are real sticky. It's next to impossible to hire someone with a criminal record, even if they turned their life around years ago.

I pivoted to a straight-up pizza joint. I'd still hire formerly incarcerated people to give them stable jobs, and I'd give them free legal support, and even housing right above the shop if they needed it. But no kids would be involved. I started hiring my recovery clients to renovate the building's plumbing and electricity, and I was securing the licenses and inspections necessary to open a restaurant. I didn't know a thing about cooking or the restaurant industry, so I brought on a promising young chef to run the kitchen.

At the time, I was also a Temple University student pursuing a degree in Criminal Justice. I'd always been intrigued by the law, how it works, and how people fall on the wrong side of it. I thought that by understanding the criminal justice system, I could better help former addicts and formerly incarcerated people stay out of trouble, stay out of jail, and get back on their feet. Did you know that more than 44 percent of former inmates in the United States end up returning to prison within one year of their release? America has one of the highest recidivism rates in the world. It's even higher in Philly, where it's near 65 percent. That's one of the reasons I started Down North Pizza.

When I graduated with a B.A. in May 2018, Down North was just starting to come together. Legacy House had grown into a network of thirteen recovery houses all over Pennsylvania, New Jersey, and Delaware. My real estate business, Prestige Worldwide, was also thriving: we were renovating twenty properties in North and West Philly into useful housing and businesses for the community. I was finally having a positive impact on a wider scale, just like my dad did. I was a happily married man, too, with a wife and three kids at home.

THE LONG ARM OF THE LAW

That's when I got indicted. Clear out of nowhere! In spring 2019, Liberation Way, the treatment center that was contracting my recovery-house business, was named in a federal insurance fraud investigation. I got wrapped up in the case. I was just a contractor in the situation, but it seems I was doing business with the wrong people. The whole thing ended up being a landmark case that changed the laws on how treatment centers bill insurance companies. To resolve things, I was forced to take a plea deal. My lawyer, Brandi L. McLaughlin, did a great job cutting my restitution down from $1.5 million to $800,000 and in reducing my jail sentence from twenty-three months in federal prison to twelve months on house arrest. But still, the situation was absolutely devastating.

That whole mess threw my life sideways. It put Down North on ice for months. This was in June 2020, when the world was on lockdown and falling apart from the pandemic. I had just two weeks to find a new apartment or I'd be forced to go upstate to prison. I managed to find one, and my house arrest started on June 26, which happens to be my wedding anniversary. As of that day, I lived alone, away from my wife and kids, for over a year. I wore an ankle monitor and could leave the apartment only for work. After all the years I'd put into understanding the criminal justice system to help former addicts and formerly incarcerated folks stay out of jail, I felt totally blindsided. Broken. My freedom was completely stripped. It was the end of my recovery-house business, and I could barely work on my real estate business. The whole thing made it near impossible to be a good husband and father.

ON A MISSION

This all happened right around the time George Floyd was murdered and social consciousness kicked into high gear. I thought long and hard about helping brothers and sisters in my community stay off drugs and alcohol, off the streets, and out of jail. Now I had first-hand knowledge of how hard it is to get back on your feet after incarceration. Giving up on Down North was not an option. Quite the opposite. My indictment and house arrest only strengthened my resolve to get this pizza shop open. It might sound crazy, but I was determined to open a pizza restaurant in 2020, at a time when 90,000 restaurants across the country were closing permanently because of the pandemic. I had to pursue this mission, even if odds were against us. It's just too important.

Everything I went through deepened my compassion for formerly incarcerated people. When you have a criminal record, no one wants to hire you. When you're on parole with an ankle monitor, you can barely move around town to get anything done, and you can work only certain hours. You're not even allowed to talk to certain people. It's almost like the system doesn't want you to bounce back.

But all those years employing formerly addicted and formerly incarcerated men and women taught me something. These are some of the hardest-working folks you'll ever meet. Most come out the other side determined to prove the world wrong. They get released from jail or treatment programs with no job, no car, often no skills, and sometimes no friends or family. They work hard to find what few jobs are available to them, and when they do get a job, they take a bus to and from work every day. They are determined to show the world "Yes, I made a mistake in life, but you made a mistake overlooking me." The Down North mission came from me thinking, *Just imagine if you humanize these people, if you give them a second chance, help them get back on their feet in a positive, supportive environment . . . the things they could achieve. . . .*

HOPE IS AN ACTION

My father taught me one of the most important lessons: hope is an action, not a feeling. During my house arrest, that thought motivated me to kick my life's work into high gear. In March 2021, we opened Down North, a pizza shop that's exclusively owned and operated by formerly incarcerated people. The organization has been "slangin' pies and savin' lives" ever since. All our work, collaborations, community outreach, and award-winning pizzas have a single purpose: to reduce recidivism rates in underserved communities, not only in Philadelphia but also around the country. I am beyond grateful to everyone who has supported this mission. Some folks do it simply by buying and enjoying our food. Some donate to the Down North Foundation (**downnorthfoundation.org**). Maybe you'll do it by making a few recipes in this book, reading the stories, and broadening your awareness. Maybe you'll get more active in your own community (check out "How You Can Help," page 206). However you do it, we thank you. In a country with the largest known prison population in the world—more than 5 million people under supervision by the criminal justice system—it'll take folks from all walks of life to make any significant change, to look past the prejudice, to see the humanity in all of us, and to give Americans who've served their time a second chance.

—MUHAMMAD ABDUL-HADI

MARC VETRI

BEEF SHANK RAGÙ, SMOKED SCAMORZA, AND HORSERADISH PIZZA

When Muhammad started his "Match Made in Philly" collabs, I was honored to be the first one. Giving guys a second chance after they come out of prison is just the right thing to do. At the time, Down North wasn't fully open yet. They were gearing up for it, doing popups. When I showed up, their mixer wasn't working and only one oven was operational. No problem. We're chefs. We figure it out!

I brought my own dough (what you see in the photo here) and made it in a square shape like the Down North pizzas. Beef was the only meat I could use because Down North is halal. At the time, we had a beef shank ragù with pappardelle on the menu at Vetri Vegas, and I figured it'd be a slam-dunk pizza topping, especially with some smoked scamorza and fresh grated horseradish for the finish. Everybody loved it, and I was psyched to be part of such an important restaurant opening in my hometown.

BEEF SHANK RAGÙ

2 cross-cut beef shanks (about 2 pounds)

Kosher salt and freshly ground black pepper

About 1 cup all-purpose flour

3 tablespoons canola oil

3 tablespoons unsalted butter

1 medium carrot, sliced about ⅛ inch thick (about 1 cup)

½ medium yellow onion, halved and thinly sliced (about ½ cup)

1 medium garlic clove, sliced

½ small celery stalk, sliced about ⅛ inch thick (about ¼ cup)

2 tablespoons finely chopped fresh flat-leaf parsley

1 cup diced canned tomatoes with juice

1½ cups dry red wine

4 to 5 cups veal stock or chicken stock

Cook the beef shanks: Preheat the oven to 350°F. Season the beef shanks all over with salt and pepper, then dredge in the flour until well coated.

Heat the oil in a Dutch oven or medium ovenproof pot or cast-iron pan over medium-high heat. Add the shanks and sear until browned all over, 8 to 10 minutes total, adding the butter toward the end of cooking and spooning the melted butter over the shanks until they become deep brown (don't let the butter burn). Remove the seared meat to a plate.

Add the carrot, onion, garlic, and celery and cook over medium heat until the vegetables are caramelized, 4 to 5 minutes, stirring to prevent burning. Add the parsley and tomatoes, and cook until the tomatoes break down a bit and look rust-colored, about 5 minutes. Pour in the wine and cook until the liquid thickens slightly, about 5 minutes. Stir in 4 cups of stock, then return the meat to the pot, burying it in the liquid. Cover and cook in the oven until a fork easily slides into the meat, 2½ to 3 hours.

When the beef is fork-tender, remove the pot from the oven and let the meat cool in the liquid, covered. When cool, remove the meat from the liquid and finely dice it (discard any tough connective tissue), then place in a large bowl. Scoop the marrow from the bones and mix it into the meat (or spread it on toast). Discard the bones. (The shanks can be made ahead, chilled for up to 4 days, and gently reheated before using.)

Make the sofrito: Heat the olive oil in a small skillet over medium-low heat. Add the leek and cook until it is translucent but not browned, 3 to 4 minutes, stirring often to prevent browning. Turn the heat to medium, add the minced garlic, and cook until fragrant and light gold in color, just a minute or two. Add the celery and parsley, and sauté until the celery is tender but still has a bite, about 2 minutes. Season with salt, black pepper, and red pepper flakes until it tastes good to you. Remove from the heat, cover, and set aside.

Finish the sauce: Puree the liquid still in the pot from cooking the shanks by using a stick blender or upright blender (or fit a food mill with the small die, set over a large bowl, and run the liquid through the mill). The consistency should be like thick tomato sauce. If it's too thick, add more stock; if too thin, simmer briefly. Taste and season with salt and pepper until it tastes good to you. Fold the sofrito into the sauce and set aside.

Preheat the oven: If you have a pizza oven, preheat it to 700°F. In a regular home oven, set the temperature to 500° or 550°F, with the convection setting on if you have it, and put a baking stone or baking steel on a top rack of the oven set 6 to 8 inches below the heat. Preheat the oven for 1 hour.

SOFRITO

2 tablespoons extra-virgin olive oil

½ leek, white part only, trimmed, cleaned, and sliced (about ¼ cup)

2 medium garlic cloves, minced

1 large celery stalk, diced (about ½ cup)

2 tablespoons finely chopped fresh flat-leaf parsley

Kosher salt and freshly ground black pepper

Pinch of red pepper flakes

FOR THE PIZZA

1¼ cups shredded low-moisture whole-milk mozzarella

1¼ cups shredded smoked scamorza cheese

1 Down North Pizza Crust (page 30), parbaked in the pan

1 to 2 tablespoons finely grated fresh horseradish

Prep the pizza: In a large bowl, mix the mozz and scamorza. Scatter the cheese blend evenly over the parbaked crust in the pan. Make sure it's pushed to the edges. You want a good amount of cheese touching the pan to create a crispy "fence" all around the edges. Scatter the diced beef over the cheese until you can barely see the cheese. (Snack on any extra meat.)

Bake: Slide the pan onto the baking stone or steel and cook until the edges of the pizza are brown, 10 to 15 minutes. In a home oven, if the edges aren't looking dark brown after 10 minutes, switch on the broiler setting. (With electric ovens, you may have to open the oven door for 10 seconds to make sure the broiler turns on.) Continue cooking for a few minutes until the pizza edges are dark brown but not burnt. Watch it like a hawk!

Slice and finish: Remove the pan from the oven and put it on a heatproof surface. Run a wide metal spatula around the edges of the pan to loosen the pizza, then use the spatula to pop out the pizza and move it to a cutting board. Let it cool for a minute, then slice into 6 pieces. Spoon the ragù in wide, diagonal stripes over the pizza. Garnish with the grated fresh horseradish. Note that this pizza will look a little different than what you see in the photo on page 145 because this recipe uses the Down North Pizza dough and the pizza is baked in a pizza pan rather than directly on a stone like the pizza in the photo.

2010s This decade is marked by expanded mass incarceration and mass surveillance with community corrections, community supervision, probation, parole, and various other practices used to control formerly incarcerated people in and around their communities.[97,98,99,100,101]

147

MICHAEL SOLOMONOV

HARISSA CHICKEN SCHNITZEL PIZZA

Our former chef at K'Far, Tim Mavour, had the idea to make a buffalo sauce enhanced with harissa, the highly seasoned North African chile paste, and marry it to a crispy schnitzel-topped pizza. We added whole cumin seeds in the breading for a bit of crunchy spice and some super-quick-to-make pickled celery on top for an extra hit of acid. We also pickle-brine the chicken to brighten up all the deep flavors. This combo was a hit at Down North when we collaborated with Muhammad in the spring of 2021. Though I was never incarcerated, as a recovering drug addict, I know the power of second chances. I'm still alive, thanks to the second chances that my community gave me. When there's a strong support network, people can change, and that's exactly what Down North provides. This place embodies the Philly spirit, the belief that you can—and *will*—make a comeback.

CHICKEN SCHNITZEL

8 ounces boneless, skinless chicken thighs (about 2 thighs)

About 1½ cups pickle brine from a jar of cucumber dill pickles

1 cup all-purpose flour

1 large egg

1½ cups panko crumbs

1 tablespoon cumin seeds

1 teaspoon kosher salt

2 quarts canola oil

Marinate the chicken: Add the chicken thighs to an empty pickle jar or bowl and cover with the pickle brine. Cover the jar and let sit in the refrigerator for 4 to 6 hours.

Preheat the oven. If you have a pizza oven, preheat it to 700°F. In a home oven, set the temperature to 500° or 550°F, with the convection setting on if you have it, and put a baking stone or baking steel on a top rack of the oven set 6 to 8 inches below the heat. Preheat the oven for 1 hour.

Make the pickled celery: Place the celery in a small bowl and season with the salt, tossing to coat. Let the celery sit at room temperature for at least 1 hour or up to 4 hours. At that point, stir in the lemon juice.

Make the Harissa Buffalo Sauce: Add the butter and brown sugar to a medium saucepan set over medium-low heat. Stir often until melted, about

QUICK PICKLED CELERY

2 celery stalks, thinly sliced crosswise (about 1 cup)

1 teaspoon kosher salt

Juice of 1 lemon

HARISSA BUFFALO SAUCE

2 tablespoons unsalted butter

1½ tablespoons (packed) dark brown sugar

1½ cups Frank's RedHot Buffalo Wings Sauce

½ tablespoon honey

½ tablespoon distilled white vinegar

2 medium garlic cloves, minced

2 tablespoons ground Aleppo pepper

1 teaspoon ground cumin

1 teaspoon ground coriander

FOR THE PIZZA

¾ cup shredded low-moisture whole-milk mozzarella

¾ cup shredded provolone cheese

¾ cup shredded sharp white cheddar cheese

1 Down North Pizza Crust (page 30), parbaked in the pan

2 minutes (or microwave in a microwave-safe medium bowl). Then remove from the heat and whisk in the Frank's sauce, honey, vinegar, garlic, Aleppo pepper, cumin, and coriander. Use immediately or keep at room temperature until ready to use, up to a few hours.

Make the schnitzel: Add the flour to a medium bowl. Whisk the egg in another medium bowl. In a third bowl, whisk together the panko, cumin seeds, and salt. Clip a candy or deep-fry thermometer to an enameled cast-iron pot or other frying pot, then add the canola oil. Heat the oil over medium-low until it reaches 350°F.

Meanwhile, dredge each chicken thigh first in flour to coat well, then in the egg to coat, then in the panko. (To avoid breading your fingers, use one hand for dipping into the dry ingredients and one for dipping into the wet.) As each thigh is done, transfer it to a baking sheet.

When the oil reaches 350°F, carefully slip in the breaded chicken thighs and fry, in batches if necessary to avoid crowding, until golden brown and the internal temperature reaches 165°F in the thickest part, 3 to 4 minutes (test by removing the chicken thigh from the oil with tongs and inserting an instant-read thermometer). Transfer the thighs to paper towels to drain.

Toss the chicken thighs with the Harissa Buffalo Sauce to coat evenly, then cut the chicken into bite-sized pieces. (You'll have some sauce left over—set it aside to drizzle over the pizza.)

Prep the pizza: In a medium bowl, mix the mozz, provolone, and cheddar cheeses. Spread the cheese mix evenly over the parbaked crust in the pan, and make sure it's pushed all the way to the edges. You want a good amount of cheese touching the pan to create a crispy "fence" all around the edges. Spread the chicken pieces over the cheese so you can barely see any cheese.

Bake: Slide the pan onto the baking stone or steel and cook until the edges of the pizza are dark brown, 10 to 15 minutes. In a home oven, if the edges aren't looking dark brown after 10 minutes, switch on the broiler setting. (With electric ovens, you may have to open the oven door for 10 seconds to make sure the broiler turns on.) Continue cooking for a few minutes, until the pizza edges are dark brown but not burnt. Watch it like a hawk!

Slice and finish: Remove the pan from the oven and put it on a heatproof surface. Scatter about ⅓ cup of the pickled celery on the pizza (nibble on any leftovers). Run a wide metal spatula around the edges of the pan to loosen the pizza, then use the spatula to pop out the pizza and move it to a cutting board. Let it cool for a minute, then slice into 6 pieces. Spoon the extra Harissa Buffalo Sauce in diagonal stripes over the pizza and enjoy.

APRIL 23, 2010   In Arizona, Senate Bill 1070 seeks to deputize local police as immigration enforcement officers, formalizing racial profiling of Latinx individuals or anyone sounding and looking seemingly "foreign."[102,103,104,105]

the game

If you're short on time, you could cheat and buy some fried chicken thighs instead of making the chicken yourself. Chop the meat from 2 fried chicken thighs (skin and bones removed, if not skinless and boneless) and toss with the sauce as directed. After you spread the chicken on the pizza, sprinkle on about a teaspoon or so of whole cumin seeds.

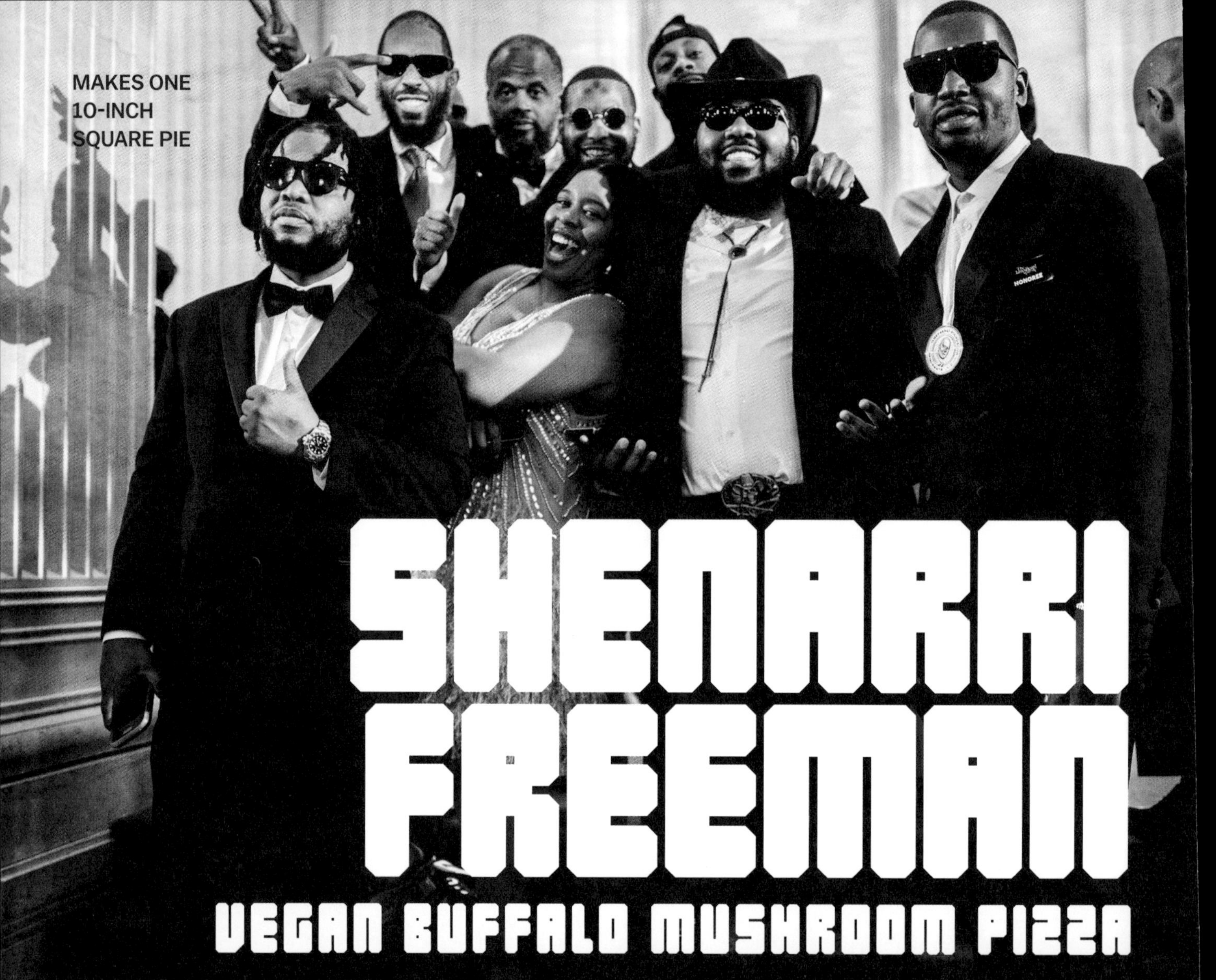

MAKES ONE
10-INCH
SQUARE PIE

SHENARRI FREEMAN

VEGAN BUFFALO MUSHROOM PIZZA

I met Muhammad and Mike in 2022, when Down North and Cadence, my restaurant in New York City, were both on a bunch of restaurant best-of lists.
I'm always looking to collaborate, and now I'm pretty glued to the hip with these guys, cooking and traveling together as friends. In August 2023, during Black-Owned Business Month, the James Beard Foundation reached out asking if I'd like to be a chef-in-residence at their Platform venue at Pier 57 in New York. I decided to extend the invitation to Mike, and we sold out with our vegan pizza collab. This one's inspired by something I grew up eating in Richmond, Virginia: buffalo chicken sandwiches. I sauté shredded oyster mushrooms and pile them onto Mike's bomb-ass pizza crust, with a vegan buffalo sauce, celery, and red onions. When it comes out of the oven, some fresh arugula and a vegan ranch dressing bring the whole thing together.

8 ounces fresh oyster mushrooms

Extra-virgin olive oil

Kosher salt and freshly ground black pepper

RANCH DRESSING

½ cup vegan mayonnaise, preferably soy-free

1½ teaspoons garlic powder

1½ teaspoons onion powder

1½ teaspoons parsley flakes

4 teaspoons fresh lemon juice

Kosher salt

BUFFALO SAUCE

⅓ cup sriracha sauce

1 tablespoon vegan butter, melted

1 teaspoon apple cider vinegar

FOR THE PIZZA

1 Down North Pizza Crust (page 30), parbaked in the pan

1 small red onion, halved and thinly sliced (about ½ cup)

1 celery stalk, thinly sliced crosswise (about ½ cup)

1 cup baby arugula leaves

Preheat the oven: If you have a pizza oven, preheat it to 700°F. In a home oven, set the temperature to 500° or 550°F, with the convection setting on if you have it, and put a baking stone or baking steel on a top rack of the oven set 6 to 8 inches below the heat. Preheat the oven for 1 hour.

Prep the mushrooms: Trim away any dirty bits from the bases of the mushroom clusters, then pull apart the stems and caps in shreds. If pieces are large, you can thinly slice the caps with a knife.

Heat a medium skillet over medium heat and swirl in a little olive oil. Add the mushrooms and cook until some of the water evaporates out of them and they're just starting to brown but are still plump, juicy, and meaty, 4 to 5 minutes with some stirring now and then. Season very lightly with salt and pepper, then remove from the heat and set aside.

Make the ranch dressing: In a spouted cup, whisk together the mayo, garlic powder, onion powder, parsley flakes, lemon juice, and ¾ teaspoon salt. Pour the dressing into a small squeeze bottle and set aside.

Make the buffalo sauce: In a cup or small bowl, whisk together the sriracha, melted butter, and vinegar. Pour the sauce over the mushrooms in the pan and toss to coat well.

Prep and bake the pizza: Spread the crust with the sautéed mushrooms, red onion strips, and celery half-moons. Slide the pan onto the baking stone or steel and cook until the edges of the pizza are dark brown, 10 to 15 minutes. In a home oven, if the edges aren't looking dark brown after 10 minutes, switch on the broiler setting. (With electric ovens, you may have to open the oven door for 10 seconds to make sure the broiler turns on.) Continue cooking for a few minutes, until the pizza edges are dark brown but not burnt. Watch it like a hawk!

Slice and finish: Remove the pan from the oven and put it on a heatproof surface. Run a wide metal spatula around the edges of the pan to loosen the pizza, then use the spatula to pop out the pizza and move it to a cutting board. Let it cool for a minute, then slice into 6 pieces. Scatter the arugula over the top, then squirt the ranch dressing in diagonal stripes over the greens. Grab a slice and have at it!

remix

CHEESY VEGAN BUFFALO MUSHROOM PIZZA: Spread a thin layer of vegan mayo (a couple tablespoons) over the parbaked crust, then scatter 2¼ cups shredded vegan mozzarella over the top, pushing the cheese all the way to the edges. Spread the mushrooms, red onion, and celery over the mozz and bake. For the finish, top with the arugula and ranch dressing as directed, and add 2 to 3 tablespoons grated vegan parmesan, if you like.

AUGUST 3, 2010 Congress passes the Fair Sentencing Act, which reduces the sentencing disparity between crack and powder cocaine to a ratio of 18:1, which was originally set at 100:1 in 1986 and drove racial sentencing disparities.[106,107]

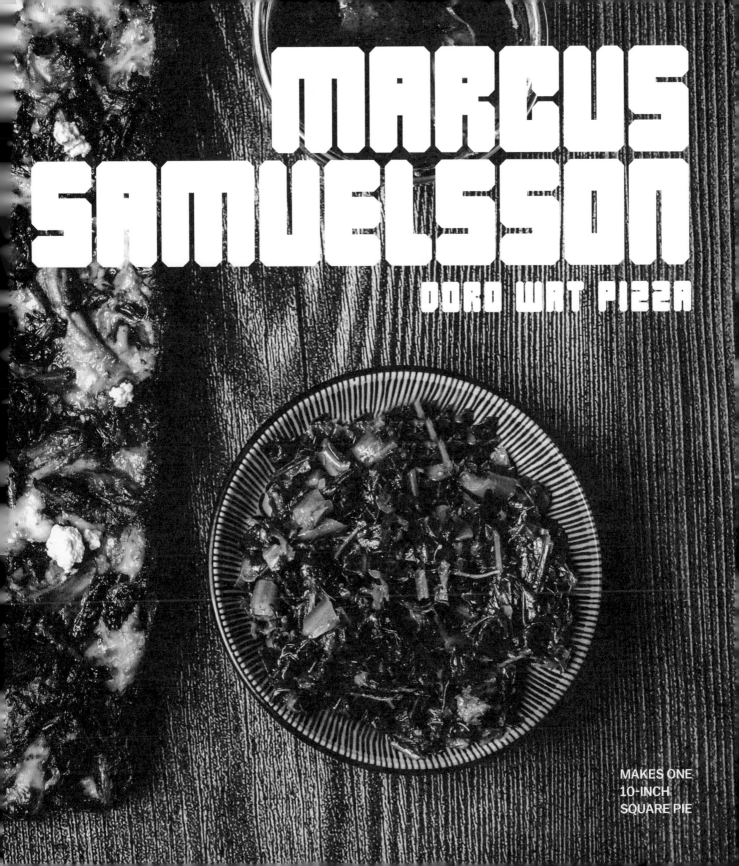

MARCUS SAMUELSSON

DORO WAT PIZZA

MAKES ONE
10-INCH
SQUARE PIE

Spicy berbere is perhaps the quintessential seasoning of Ethiopia, and doro wat is the quintessential stew. In this pizza, you taste them both. Ethiopian stews are traditionally scooped up with injera, a flatbread made from teff grain. Here, the crispy, airy Down North Pizza Crust takes its place, serving as the base for the spicy chicken stew, slow-braised collard greens, and ayib, a fresh homemade Ethiopian cheese. Taste these flavors and you will taste the soul of my Ethiopian roots. You will also get a taste of my commitment to helping underserved youth and formerly incarcerated people. My mother died when I was three, and I was adopted by a Swedish family who nurtured my love of cooking. Without their love and generosity, I never would have had the good fortune to become an American chef and to collaborate with organizations like Down North, dedicated to helping Black Americans recover from mass incarceration by welcoming them into the hospitality industry.

DORO WAT

1 boneless, skinless chicken thigh (about 4 ounces)

¼ teaspoon kosher salt

⅛ teaspoon freshly ground black pepper

4 tablespoons (½ stick) unsalted butter

½ teaspoon ground fenugreek

½ large red onion, diced (about ¾ cup)

1 (3-inch) piece fresh ginger, peeled and minced (about 2½ tablespoons)

10 large garlic cloves, minced (about 2½ tablespoons)

1 generous tablespoon berbere seasoning

1 cup canned crushed tomatoes

AYIB

2 cups whole buttermilk

½ cup plain whole-milk yogurt

1¼ teaspoons kosher salt

Make the doro wat: Season the chicken all over with the salt and pepper.

Heat the butter and fenugreek in a medium cast-iron or heatproof pot (with heatproof lid) over medium heat. Once the butter has melted, stir in the onion, ginger, and garlic. Decrease the heat to low, cover, and cook, uncovering to stir occasionally, until the vegetables are very tender, about 30 minutes. Meanwhile, preheat the oven to 350°F.

Uncover and cook until the vegetables look browned and caramelized, 10 to 15 minutes more. Stir the berbere into the vegetables and cook for 2 to 3 minutes. Stir in the tomatoes, bring to a simmer, and cook about 5 minutes. Add the chicken and fold the sauce over it. Cover and braise in the oven until the chicken is cooked through and tender, 25 to 30 minutes. Remove from the oven and leave to cool in the pot.

Once cool enough to handle, scoop out and set aside about ¾ cup sauce. Remove the chicken from the pot and use two forks to shred, then fold the chicken shreds back into the sauce. You should have about 2 cups doro wat in the pot. Use immediately or refrigerate in a covered container for up to 3 days.

Make the ayib: Whisk together the buttermilk, yogurt, and salt in a medium saucepan and bring to a gentle simmer over medium heat. Decrease the heat to low, and simmer gently until curds form, about 30 minutes. Turn off the heat and let everything settle for at least 30 minutes or up to 1 hour.

Strain the ayib through a fine-mesh strainer until about three-fourths of the liquid is expelled. Use the pulp immediately or refrigerate in a covered container for up to 3 days.

COLLARD GREENS

2 tablespoons unsalted butter

½ small yellow onion, diced small (about ⅓ cup)

1 small garlic clove, thinly sliced

1 bunch collard greens (about 8 ounces), ribs removed and leaves coarsely chopped

1½ cups chicken stock

6 tablespoons pure maple syrup

¼ cup Dijon mustard

¼ cup apple cider vinegar

1 tablespoon smoked paprika

1 tablespoon granulated onion

1 tablespoon granulated garlic

Pinch of red pepper flakes

1 teaspoon kosher salt, plus more as needed

Freshly ground black pepper

FOR THE PIZZA

1 Down North Pizza Crust (page 30), parbaked in the pan

3 large fresh basil leaves, chopped (optional)

1 hardboiled egg, halved lengthwise

About 1 tablespoon extra-virgin olive oil

Make the collards: Melt the butter in a medium saucepan over medium heat. Add the onion and garlic and cook until soft, about 5 minutes, stirring now and then. Stir in the collards, stock, maple syrup, mustard, vinegar, smoked paprika, granulated onion and granulated garlic, red pepper flakes, and salt. Cook over medium heat until the collards are tender, about 45 minutes, stirring occasionally. Remove from the heat, taste, and add additional salt and some pepper until it tastes good to you. You should have about 2 cups.

Preheat the oven: If you have a pizza oven, preheat it to 700°F. In a home oven, set the temperature to 500° or 550°F, with the convection setting on if you have it, and put a baking stone or baking steel on a top rack of the oven set 6 to 8 inches below the heat. Preheat the oven for 1 hour.

Prep the pizza: Use a slotted spoon to scoop up about 1¼ cups of the doro wat, draining it a bit and then spreading it evenly over the parbaked crust. Use another slotted spoon to scoop up a generous ½ cup of the braised collards, also draining a bit, then spreading them evenly over the doro wat. Crumble a generous ½ cup of the ayib evenly over the top.

Bake: Slide the pan onto the baking stone or steel and cook until the edges of the pizza are brown, 10 to 15 minutes. In a home oven, if the edges aren't looking dark brown after 10 minutes, switch on the broiler setting. (With electric ovens, you may have to open the oven door for 10 seconds to make sure the broiler turns on.) Continue cooking for a few minutes, until the pizza edges are dark brown but not burnt. Watch it like a hawk!

Slice and finish: Remove the pan from the oven and put it on a heatproof surface. Run a wide metal spatula around the edges of the pan to loosen the pizza, then use the spatula to pop out the pizza and move it to a cutting board. Let it cool for a minute, then slice into 6 pieces. Spoon the reserved doro wat sauce in diagonal stripes over the pizza and garnish with fresh basil (if using), the hardboiled egg halves, and the olive oil.

OCTOBER 2014 As of this date, the United States is commonly cited as the world's leader in incarceration. With only 5 percent of the world population, the United States disproportionately detains close to 25 percent of the world's incarcerated: 2.2 million people.[108]

MAKES
ONE
10-INCH
SQUARE
PIE

REEM ASSIL
PALI CALI PIZZA

With sumac-seasoned braised chicken, caramelized onion puree, and pomegranate molasses, this pizza embodies the earthy, sharp flavors of Palestine, my homeland. A garnish of fresh arugula gives it a California spin and speaks to everything I am trying to achieve with my cooking. I see food as a medium for building community across cultures, generations, and experiences. I was thrilled when Mike asked me to collab on a pizza with him. Down North is doing amazing work building community and creating opportunities for formerly incarcerated people. I believe that all of us have a role to play in providing opportunities to marginalized communities through hiring locally, providing living wages, and nurturing leadership. I'm proud to join Down North in this effort.

BRAISED CHICKEN

8 ounces boneless, skinless chicken thighs (about 2 thighs)

1½ tablespoons sumac

2½ teaspoons kosher salt

4 tablespoons extra-virgin olive oil

3 large yellow onions, halved and thinly sliced (about 4½ cups)

PICKLED RED ONION

¼ cup apple cider vinegar

¼ cup water

1 tablespoon lemon juice

4 teaspoons kosher salt

1½ teaspoons sumac

½ red onion, halved and thinly sliced (about ½ cup)

YELLOW ONION PUREE

¾ teaspoon pomegranate molasses

1 teaspoon kosher salt

¼ teaspoon ground black pepper

2 tablespoons extra-virgin olive oil

FOR THE PIZZA

1 Down North Pizza Crust (page 30), parbaked in the pan

2 cups shredded low-moisture, whole-milk mozzarella

About ⅓ cup arugula leaves

Marinate and bake the chicken: Put the chicken thighs in a medium bowl and scatter on the sumac and 1½ teaspoons of salt. Rub the seasoning into the chicken, cover, and let sit for 2 hours at room temperature or refrigerate overnight.

Preheat the oven to 300°F. Heat 2 tablespoons of olive oil in a large, heavy skillet over medium heat. Add the yellow onions and the remaining teaspoon of salt and sauté until they're translucent, 4 to 5 minutes, stirring a few times. Reduce the heat to low and cook until the onions are browned and caramelized, about 30 minutes, stirring and evening out the onions in the pan every 10 minutes. Set aside ¾ cup of the caramelized onions to make the yellow onion puree.

Spread the remaining caramelized onions in a small baking dish. Drizzle with the remaining 2 tablespoons of olive oil, then arrange the chicken in the dish over the onions in a single layer. Cover with aluminum foil and bake until the chicken pulls apart easily with a fork (165°F internal temperature on an instant-read thermometer), 50 to 60 minutes. Remove the dish from the oven and shred the chicken with a fork, then stir the chicken into the onions until well mixed. Set aside and use within 2 hours. Or refrigerate in a covered container for up to 2 days.

Pickle the red onion: Combine the vinegar, water, lemon juice, salt, and sumac in a medium bowl. Stir in the red onion, immersing the slices completely. Cover and let sit at room temperature for up to 2 hours. Or refrigerate in a covered container for up to 2 weeks.

Make the yellow onion puree: Combine the reserved ¾ cup caramelized yellow onions with the pomegranate molasses, salt, and pepper. Blend to a smooth puree with a stick blender. Gradually drizzle in the olive oil and continue blending until the puree is thick and emulsified.

Preheat the oven: If you have a pizza oven, preheat it to 700°F. In a home oven, set the temperature to 500° or 550°F, with the convection setting on if you have it, and put a baking stone or baking steel on a top rack of the oven set 6 to 8 inches below the heat. Preheat the oven for 1 hour.

Prep the pizza and bake: Spread the yellow onion puree over the parbaked crust in the pan, then scatter on the mozz. Arrange the braised chicken over the top. Slide the pan onto the baking stone or steel and cook until the edges of the pizza are brown, 10 to 15 minutes. In a home oven, if the edges aren't looking dark brown after 10 minutes, switch on the broiler setting. (With electric ovens, you may have to open the oven door for 10 seconds to make sure the broiler turns on.) Continue cooking for a few minutes, until the pizza edges are dark brown but not burnt. Watch it like a hawk!

Slice and finish: Remove the pan from the oven and put it on a heatproof surface. Run a wide metal spatula around the edges of the pan to loosen the pizza, then use the spatula to pop out the pizza and move it to a cutting board. Let it cool for a minute, then slice into 6 pieces. Scatter the arugula leaves and the pickled red onion over the top.

MAY 2015 The city of Chicago establishes a reparations fund to atone for police violence and torture mostly experienced by Black people from the 1970s through the 1990s.[109]

159

NICOLE + MICI

MAKES ONE
10-INCH
SQUARE PIE

AEL NICHOLAS

RAW AND UNCUT

Our collab with Down North happened so naturally. Philadelphia's Down North stands as a beacon of empowerment, being owned and operated exclusively by formerly incarcerated individuals; meanwhile, Aunts et Uncles in Brooklyn's Little Caribbean is a haven for innovative food that's as healthy as it is flavorful, opening its doors to foster the dreams and aspirations of the community's visionaries. This recipe uniquely weaves together our collective culinary talents: a vegan take on a Jamaican beef patty in the form of a Philly-style pizza. The crust hints at fluffy Jamaican coco bread, essentially the Down North crust made with coconut essence. The Tivoli meat topping nods to Tivoli Gardens in Kingston and is our plant-based remix of a Jamaican beef patty filling. Chef Mike made a turmeric crumble for some crunch on top, and we made the Elo sauce for the finish, a spicy mayonnaise named after our only living relative with the original recipe for Caribbean pepper sauce that goes back generations in the family. Oh, and the name, "Raw and Uncut"? That's Mike Carter's genius at work: it's the first collab song between Jay-Z and Beanie Sigel. Another example of New York and Philly comin' together in perfect harmony.

TURMERIC CRUMBLE

½ cup all-purpose flour

½ teaspoon ground turmeric

½ teaspoon Jamaican curry powder

1 tablespoon vegetable shortening

1 to 3 tablespoons ice water

FRESH TIVOLI SEASONING

1 large scallion, white and green parts trimmed and finely chopped (about 1 tablespoon)

2 to 3 large garlic cloves, finely chopped (about 1 tablespoon)

1 (2-inch) piece fresh ginger, peeled and finely chopped (generous 1 tablespoon)

1 to 2 fresh mild Jamaican pimento peppers (a.k.a. seasoning peppers) or cherry peppers, seeded and finely chopped (about 1 tablespoon)

¼ small fresh Scotch bonnet chile, finely chopped

TIVOLI MEAT

1 pound Beyond Beef, thawed if frozen

Olive oil or vegetable oil, for frying

¼ small yellow onion, finely chopped (about 3 tablespoons)

6 large garlic cloves, finely chopped (about 3 tablespoons)

Make the turmeric crumble: Preheat the oven to 400°F. In a small bowl, mix the flour, turmeric, and curry powder. Add the shortening and use your fingers or a fork to work the fat into the flour. Work quickly, but don't be too aggressive: you don't want the shortening to melt. When well incorporated, you should see irregular pieces of fat strewn throughout the flour.

Stir 1 tablespoon of ice water into the flour mixture, then continue stirring in a tablespoon of water at a time, adding just enough water for the dough to stick to itself when you pinch up a piece of dough with your finger (you may not need all the ice water). The dough should still look more dry than wet. Form it into a ball, cover, and chill for 30 minutes.

Put the chilled dough on a piece of parchment and roll it out with a lightly floured pin to a circle that's between ⅛ and ¼ inch thick. Transfer the dough round along with the parchment to a large sheet pan and bake until it's dry and crisp, about 15 minutes. Remove from the oven and set aside to cool completely, then bust it up by hand into small, irregular shards.

Preheat the oven: If you have a pizza oven, preheat it to 700°F. If using a home oven, set the temperature to 500° or 550°F, with the convection setting on if you have it, and put a baking stone or baking steel on a top rack of the oven set 6 to 8 inches below the heat. Preheat the oven for 1 hour.

Make the Tivoli seasoning: Place the scallion, garlic, ginger, pimento peppers, and Scotch bonnet chile on a cutting board and chop all together until finely chopped. You could also use a mini-chopper, but avoid making a puree. Set aside.

Sauté the Tivoli meat: Add the Beyond Beef and a little olive oil to a large nonstick skillet set over medium-high heat and cook until lightly browned, about 5 minutes, breaking it up with a spoon as it cooks. Stir in the onion and garlic, and cook until they are softened, about 5 minutes. Stir in 3 tablespoons of the Tivoli seasoning along with the tomato, Baron pepper sauce, rum, curry powder, cumin, allspice, black pepper, and sugar. (Save any remaining Tivoli seasoning for another use—think of it as Caribbean sofrito to add to any sauté.) Cut the heat to medium-low and simmer until the mixture holds together like an empanada filling and is still a little juicy, about 5 minutes. Taste and season with a little salt, if you think it needs it.

¼ small ripe tomato, finely chopped (about 3 tablespoons)

½ teaspoon Baron West Indian Hot Sauce or other Caribbean hot sauce

1 tablespoon Jamaican white rum (such as Wray & Nephew)

1 teaspoon Jamaican curry powder

1 teaspoon ground cumin

1 teaspoon ground allspice

½ teaspoon freshly ground black pepper

½ teaspoon sugar

Kosher salt

ELO SAUCE

½ cup vegan mayonnaise, plus some for crust

2 tablespoons Aunts et Uncles Peppa Sauce or other Caribbean hot sauce

FOR THE PIZZA

Vegan mayonnaise

1 Coco Bread Crust (page 31), parbaked in the pan

2 cups shredded vegan mozzarella

2 scallions (green part only), chopped, for garnish

Mix the Elo sauce: In a small bowl, whisk together the mayo and hot sauce. Spoon it into a small squirt bottle (optional) and set aside.

Prep the pizza: Spread a thin layer of vegan mayo over the parbaked crust in the pan, then scatter the vegan mozz evenly over the top. Make sure it's pushed to the edges. You want a good amount of cheese touching the pan to create a crispy "fence" all around the edges. Cover the whole pie with the Tivoli meat, until you can barely see the cheese. (Snack on any leftover Tivoli meat. Or serve it in tacos!)

Bake: Slide the pan onto the baking stone or steel and cook until the edges of the pizza are dark brown, 10 to 15 minutes. In a home oven, if the edges aren't looking dark brown after 10 minutes, switch on the broiler setting. (With electric ovens, you may have to open the oven door for 10 seconds to make sure the broiler turns on.) Continue cooking for a few minutes, until the pizza edges are dark brown but not burnt. Watch it like a hawk!

Slice and finish: Remove the pan from the oven and put it on a heatproof surface. Run a wide metal spatula around the edges of the pan to loosen the pizza, then use the spatula to pop out the pizza and move it to a cutting board. Let it cool for a minute, then slice into 6 pieces. Place the shards of turmeric crumble evenly over the top (use ½ cup or so), and then scatter on the scallion greens. Squeeze the Elo sauce in a diagonal zigzag over the top and dig in.

OCTOBER 2016—2017 The Standing Rock Sioux peacefully demonstrate against the construction of the Dakota Access Pipeline on the grounds that it threatens the region's water and violates Article II of the Fort Laramie Treaty, which codified the "undisturbed use and occupation" of reservation land. The demonstration results in police using water cannons, tear gas, and rubber bullets against demonstrators camped out in subzero temperatures. Activists are also subjected to coordinated surveillance and tracking involving private security, the FBI, and local law enforcement.[110,111]

WINGS +

FRIES

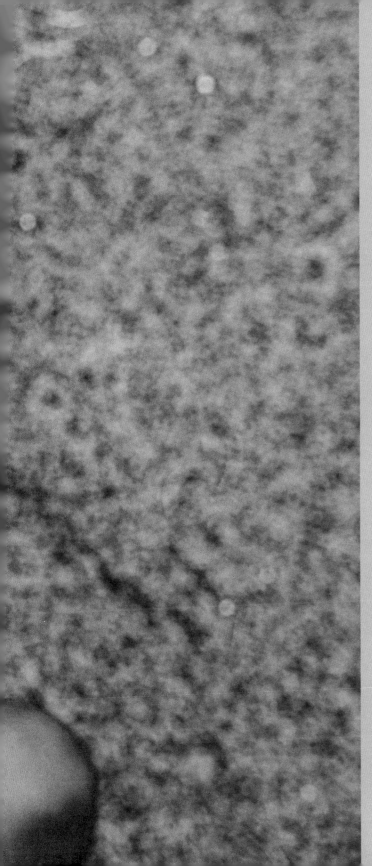

Pizza is our main thing at Down North. While the wings and fries are what we call "menu fillers," that doesn't mean they don't slap. Our Norffalo Sauce (page 35) ain't your typical wing sauce. I mix a couple different hot sauces to round out the flavor. And I season the wings with a mix of Ethiopian berbere, Old Bay, and a few other spices.

If you're tired of buffalo sauce on wings, try our spicy Flip Side BBQ Sauce (page 39), sweet Honey Chipotle Sauce (page 43), creamy Garlic-Parm Sauce (page 46), or sweet-hot Quick Thai Red Curry Sauce (page 40).

We do cauliflower wings, too. After cooking at vegan places like Vedge and V Street in Philly, I pay more attention to vegetables than your average chef. I know how good vegetables can be. Our fried cauliflower wings are crisped up with a mix of rice flour and potato starch and are seasoned with gochugaru (Korean red chili flakes). Sauce 'em how you like with the spicy Vegan Norffalo Sauce (page 35), creamy za'atar sauce (see page 175), or Quick Thai Red Curry Sauce with a sprinkle of toasted sesame seeds, Thai basil, and lime juice. You don't have to call that kind of food vegan. It's just good food.

Of course, if you love meat and cheese, you can't go wrong with our classic Norf Fries (page 176), topped with Spicy Cheese Sauce (page 45), crispy beef bacon, House BBQ Sauce (page 38), and crunchy fried shallots. Best fully loaded fries ever. —MIKE CARTER

DERRICK COBB

When I was twenty-two, I'd do anything for my crew. We looked out for each other. In early spring 1995, me and a friend went to the Gallery Mall in Center City Philadelphia. I was downstairs on the lower level just walking around, and my friend was upstairs. When I went back up, someone was chasing him. I didn't know what was happening, but I did know that I had my friend's back, and so I pulled out my gun. Looking back now, that was a bad move. But I was kinda wild back then. I just reacted and started shooting right there in the mall, without even knowing if the guy chasing my friend had a gun. People were running and ducking for cover. I can't imagine what they must have been thinking. Turns out my friend had robbed the sneaker store upstairs, and the guy I was shooting at was just the store guy chasing him. When the cops caught us, they charged me as an accessory to the robbery 'cuz I shot my gun. I spent ten years upstate at SCI Smithfield for that charge.

When I got out, I got an apartment and soon after, my girlfriend got pregnant. Bills were coming in. I was working a home-healthcare job and getting paid under the table, but my parole officer told me I had to quit that job, 'cuz when you get out of prison you have to prove that you're workin'. You have to have a paper trail. I didn't have no pay stubs. At that point, my kid was due in three and a half months. My rent was due every other day, it seemed. I was getting desperate.

Without even thinking, I threw on a wig, pulled on a hoodie, and walked into a Citizens Bank in northeast Philly, across from the old folks' home where I was workin'. I pulled out my gun and a stuff bag, and shouted at the bank people, "Give me the money! Don't do nothin' stupid!" Fifteen minutes later, I walked out with the money, and the cops were right there waiting for me. Caught me red-handed.

I got convicted for armed robbery and went to federal prison for another fifteen years. Because of that dumb decision, I pretty much missed the first fifteen years of my son's life. I knew I'd never get out of prison if I kept screwing up, so I did all my programs, sewed military uniforms, took a computer course—even took some cooking classes. I worked in the prison kitchen, too, just like I did when I was at SCI Smithfield. I also sold sandwiches on the side for extra money. And I gambled. I'd bet on anything—football, basketball, NASCAR, horse racing. Everything I won went home to take care of my son.

When I got home in 2020, I was almost fifty years old and had spent almost half my life in prison. At that point, I just wanted to be home for my son, to provide for him. I started working at Philabundance, the food bank and community kitchen that's part of Feeding America, a big hunger-relief organization. I was catering, cooking lunches and dinners for different corporations. Cooking always came easy to me. In my younger days, I was a short-order cook at places like Friendly's, Wendy's, and Bassett's Turkey, in the Reading Terminal Market, plus I cooked the whole time I was in prison.

After a few months at Philabundance, the federal probation reentry program told me about this new place called Down North Pizza. The people at this place were like me. They'd all been in prison. They were trying to stay off the streets and to maintain a good job. To live a good life. A few months after Down North opened, I started working there, cooking on the line, building and cooking pizzas and boxing 'em up. I liked working there. It was a peaceful place to come to, a good work atmosphere where you could be yourself.

To pay the bills, I worked thirty-five hours at Down North, forty hours at Philabundance, and thirty-five hours at the cafeteria at Villanova University—that's 110 hours a week. I'd come home so tired, and all I'd want to do is sit and watch a movie for two hours before going to bed. Then I'd get up and do it all over again the next day. It was bad. I was stressed. Not eating right. And I was gambling a lot.

Around May 2022, I'd been out of federal prison for a year or so and was finishing up some food prep at Philabundance when I felt a little tightness in my chest. I didn't pay it no mind and went to the casino to blow off steam. I reached out to place my bet and suddenly my chest felt like someone was stomping on my heart. I bent over to relieve the pain, and a security guard came over thinking I was having some kind of drug reaction. I got sent to Episcopal Hospital on Lehigh Avenue. I was sitting there in the waiting room for an hour, leaning forward to feel better because every time I sat up, my heart felt like it was getting twisted. About an hour later, they put some wires on my chest to check my vitals and realized I was having a heart attack the whole time. They transferred me right away to Temple University Hospital, and when they put a stent in my heart, I had a bad reaction to the medication they gave me. I almost died on the operating table. With the heart attack and the near-death situation, I guess I'm pretty lucky to be alive.

Down North has been a part of that, too. This place has been a good influence on me, showing me how to be a better father and how to take care of myself better. I'm here about four days a week, preppin' and baking pies. I also make pizzas at the Eastern State Penitentiary, the first real penitentiary in the world and one of Down North's partners. It's just a prison museum for tourists now, but we serve pizza there to thousands of visitors. It feels funny walking into the penitentiary to work. I always think, "This is the place I was trying to get away from!" I'm there for a good reason, though. Eastern State is helping get the message out there about staying out of jail.

I wish I heard that message a little sooner in my life. If I could go back in time, I'd tell my younger self, "Leave the streets alone." Thing is, when you're young, you get caught up in these situations. You're not necessarily a bad person, but maybe you're with people who take things too far. Or you get desperate and make bad decisions. That's what took away twenty-five years of my life.

I'm just glad my son got the message early. Seeing what I went through made him a better person, and his mom did a good job raising him. Derrick Jr.'s graduated from high school now and pursuing a career in architecture. He's on a totally different path than I was. I'm so thankful that I can be here now to support him. That's exactly what I'm going to keep doing.

NORFFALO WINGS

When we opened Down North, the concept was pizza, wings, fries, and shakes. We thought wings would help complete the menu, a choice for folks who don't want a whole pizza. Now I sell out of wings most days. Our signature seasoning is Ethiopian berbere mixed with Old Bay, plus a little garlic powder, onion powder, and black pepper. The process is simple: season the wings, heat your oil, fry 'em up crisp, and toss in sauce. I'm not a big salt guy. But for the Garlic-Parm, Honey Chipotle, and Quick Thai Red Curry sauce options, you may want to sprinkle a little salt on top.

3 pounds chicken wings (about 12 whole wings), or 24 chicken wing flats and drumettes

1 tablespoon garlic powder

1 tablespoon onion powder

½ tablespoon Old Bay seasoning

½ tablespoon berbere seasoning

¾ teaspoon freshly ground black pepper

About 2 quarts neutral oil, such as canola

About ½ cup Norffalo Sauce (page 35)

Cut off and discard the chicken wing tips (or save them for chicken stock), then cut each wing into 2 pieces (a flat and a drumette) through the joint where they connect. (If you bought your wings already split into flats and drumettes, skip this step.) Put the pieces in a large bowl.

In a small bowl or cup, mix the garlic powder, onion powder, Old Bay, berbere, and black pepper. Scatter the seasoning over the wings and toss to coat evenly. Set aside while you heat the oil (or cover and chill up to 8 hours).

Heat the oil in a large pot over medium heat until an instant-read thermometer reads 350°F. Fry the wings, in batches, if necessary, to prevent overcrowding, until the skins are crispy and the meat is cooked through, about 10 minutes (remove one to check it's temperature, which should be 165°F when done). Continue to check the oil temperature while frying, adjusting the heat to maintain the 350°F the whole time. When they're done, use a slotted spoon or frying spider to transfer the wings to paper towels or a big paper bag to drain.

Pour the Norffalo Sauce into a large bowl, add the just-fried wings, and toss to coat. Get 'em while they're hot!

NOVEMBER 2016 The American Public Health Association calls out law enforcement violence as a public health concern.[112,113]

remix

BBQ WINGS: Use Flip Side BBQ Sauce (page 39) or House BBQ Sauce (page 38) instead of the Norffalo Sauce.

HONEY CHIPOTLE WINGS: Use Honey Chipotle Sauce (page 43) instead of the Norffalo Sauce. BTW, these are our most popular wings.

GARLIC PARMESAN WINGS: Use Garlic-Parm Sauce (page 46) instead of the Norffalo Sauce. Garnish with some grated parmesan just before serving.

THAI CHILI WINGS: Use Quick Thai Red Curry Sauce (page 40) instead of the Norffalo Sauce, and sprinkle on 2 to 3 teaspoons toasted sesame seeds and 1 tablespoon chopped fresh cilantro just before serving.

the game

At the shop, we par-fry the wings, then flash-fry them to order. If you're having a party at home, that might help speed things up for you. Just par-fry them at 350°F until they float, 5 to 7 minutes. Use a slotted spoon or frying spider to transfer them to paper towels or a big paper bag to drain. Then refrigerate them up to 2 days. Before serving, fry again at 350°F for just a few minutes, then drain and toss in the sauce.

VEGAN NORFFALO CAULIFLOWER WINGS

For about two years, I worked at Vedge and V Street, some of the best vegan restaurants in the country (V Street closed during the pandemic). I was on prep at V Street, and we had this vegan buffalo sauce with sriracha and vegan butter. It was good on fried cauliflower, but I had an idea to take it up another level. I suggested tossin' the cauliflower in rice flour and potato starch before we fry it up, so it gets even crispier. The chef wasn't havin' it. I took what I learned there and now we make crispy cauliflower wings the way I think they should be made at Down North.

About 2 quarts neutral oil, such as canola

2 cups rice flour

½ cup potato starch

½ cup gochugaru (Korean red chili flakes; see The Game)

½ tablespoon onion powder

½ tablespoon garlic powder

1 cup soy milk

1 medium cauliflower, trimmed and cut into bite-sized florets

About ¾ cup Norffalo Sauce (page 35)

Add the oil to a large pot or deep fryer and heat until it reaches 350°F on an instant-read thermometer.

For the dredge, whisk together the rice flour, potato starch, pepper flakes, onion powder, and garlic powder in a medium bowl. Pour the soy milk into another medium bowl. Whisk about ¼ cup of the dry mix into the soy milk to thicken it so it's like a very thin batter.

Dip a few cauliflower florets at a time into the soy milk, then into the dry mix, shaking off any excess. Transfer to a wire rack and continue with the remaining florets. Carefully add them to the hot oil in batches (don't crowd them; otherwise they won't cook properly) and cook until golden brown on the outside and soft on the inside, 3 to 4 minutes, adjusting the heat as needed to maintain that 350°F frying temperature. When done, use a slotted spoon or frying spider to transfer them to paper towels or a large brown paper bag to drain.

Add the Norffalo Sauce to a large bowl. While still hot, toss the fried cauliflower wings in the sauce. Serve it up.

the game

I like to grind my Korean chili flakes to a powder to distribute the flavor better. If you're into that, a spice grinder or clean coffee mill does the job.

remix

VEGAN THAI CHILI CAULIFLOWER WINGS:
Skip the Norffalo Sauce. Instead, toss the fried wings in about ¾ cup Quick Thai Red Curry Sauce (page 40). Sprinkle with about 2 teaspoons toasted sesame seeds and about 1 tablespoon of chopped fresh Thai basil. Serve with lime wedges for squeezing.

VEGAN ZA'ATAR CAULIFLOWER WINGS:
Skip the Norffalo Sauce. Instead, in a small bowl, combine 1 cup vegan mayo, 1 tablespoon za'atar, and 1 tablespoon chopped fresh cilantro. As soon as the wings come out of the fryer, sprinkle them with about a tablespoon of za'atar, then serve with the za'atar sauce on the side.

2016 The Corrections Corporation of America generates $1.8 billion in revenue, rebrands as CoreCivic, and in early 2017, the stock escalates by 140 percent, prompting an upsurge in America's for-profit private correctional facilities market and incentivizing an increase in prisoners.[114]

SERVES
2 TO 4

NORF FRIES

This recipe uses whole potatoes that are hand-cut into sticks, held in salted water until needed, then fried, topped, and served. The toppings are what make 'em great. I love beef bacon (I don't eat pork), and ya can't go wrong with fries and bacon. Spoon on some spicy cheese sauce and crispy dried shallots, and you're in business. Look for dried fried shallots (they come in big plastic containers) in an Asian market. My favorite place in Philly is Oregon Market. H-Mart has 'em, too. Or just fry up some sliced fresh shallots yourself until they get nice and crispy.

2 large russet potatoes (about 28 ounces total), scrubbed (not peeled)

Kosher salt

About 2 quarts neutral oil, such as canola

4 to 6 slices beef bacon, cut into 1-inch squares

Dirty Salt (see The Game)

⅔ to 1 cup Spicy Cheese Sauce (page 45)

About ¼ cup Flip Side BBQ Sauce (page 39) or House BBQ Sauce (page 38)

About ¼ cup crispy dried fried shallots

Cut the potatoes into long, narrow sticks and drop 'em in a tub of cold salted water (about 1½ teaspoons kosher salt per 4 cups water). Let them hang out in the water until you need them (up to 8 hours).

Add the oil to a large pot or deep fryer and heat until it reaches 350°F on an instant-read thermometer. We like to deep-fry the bacon since the fryer is already at temperature, but you can cook the bacon in a pan or in the oven, if you prefer. If deep frying, just drop it into the oil and fry until crispy, 2 to 3 minutes, fishing it out with a spider or slotted spoon, then setting it onto paper towels to drain.

Drop your fries in the hot oil and let 'em go until they float to the surface, then get nice and crispy, 6 to 8 minutes. They may not get super-brown—just make sure they're crispy. Test one to make sure. Use a spider or slotted spoon to transfer the potatoes to paper towels or a paper bag to drain. Immediately shake on the dirty salt to taste, tossing gently to coat.

Serve up the fries on a shallow tray, topped with the bacon, cheese sauce, BBQ sauce, and fried shallots. Get 'em while they hot.

the game

I use salt and pepper so often, I mix them ahead and call it "dirty salt," which saves time. To make Dirty Salt, just mix kosher salt and ground pepper in a 7:1 ratio.

Potatoes get creamier inside and crispier outside when they are fried twice. If you have the time, you won't be disappointed by the results. To twice-fry, fry once at 350°F until the fries float, about 3 minutes, then drain and spread them out on a baking sheet to cool. Cover and chill until needed, then fry again at the same temperature until golden brown.

For extra-crispy fries, follow the directions for twice-frying (see above), but after the first fry, toss the par-fried fries in 1 to 2 tablespoons potato starch while they still have some grease on them. Get 'em coated evenly, then cool them completely, cover, and chill until needed. Fry again and they'll get nice and crunchy on the outside.

JANUARY 27, 2017 President Trump issues a Muslim ban, facilitating the systematic detainment of Muslim immigrants and travelers at airports. Widespread protests immediately ensue and police are deployed.[115,116]

remix

SPICY CHEESE FRIES: Serve the fries with the cheese sauce and nothing else.

SPICY CRAB FRIES: Strip the leafy part from about 1 ounce of kale (about 1 large leaf), then chop the greens. Drop them into the frying oil and fry until crispy, about 1 minute. Scoop out and drain on paper towels. (Or just use some store-bought crispy kale chips.) Top the fries with 3 ounces of lump crab meat, a ladle of the cheese sauce, the crispy kale, and a generous shake of Old Bay seasoning.

VEGAN WIZ FRIES

I recognize that a lot of people don't deal with dairy. That's where Vegan Wiz Sauce (page 49) comes in. This sauce gets thick and creamy from pureed rutabaga with some nutritional yeast for that cheesy, umami taste. Spoon it over some crispy fries, and I promise you won't miss the dairy. The Everything option—with toasted nori and sesame seeds—is my favorite way to bump up these cheese fries. I've never had nori on something that it didn't improve.

A lot of vegans like the Crab Fries option, too. Those get Old Bay Mushrooms (page 55) and fried kale on top, along with the Vegan Wiz Sauce. It totally slaps. And if you like twice-fried or extra-crispy fries, see The Game on page 177.

2 large russet potatoes (about 28 ounces total), scrubbed (not peeled)

Kosher salt

About 2 quarts neutral oil, such as canola

Dirty Salt (see The Game, page 177)

⅔ cup Vegan Wiz Sauce (page 49), warmed

Cut the potatoes into long, narrow sticks and drop 'em in a tub of cold salted water (about 1½ teaspoons kosher salt per 4 cups water). Let them hang out in the water until you need them (up to 8 hours).

Add the oil to a large pot or deep fryer and heat until it reaches 350°F on an instant-read thermometer. Drop the fries into the hot oil and let 'em go until they float to the surface and then get nice and crispy, 6 to 8 minutes. They may not get super-brown; just make sure they're crispy. Test one to make sure. Use a frying spider or slotted spoon to transfer them to paper towels or a paper bag to drain.

Immediately shake on the Dirty Salt to taste, tossing gently to coat. We serve up the fries in a shallow tray topped with the Vegan Wiz Sauce.

2018 Colorado bans forced prison labor; however, incarcerated individuals still experience it. Five years after the ban, incarcerated individuals in Colorado are still subject to forced labor.[117]

remix

VEGAN EVERYTHING FRIES: In addition to the Vegan Wiz Sauce, squirt on 2 to 3 tablespoons House BBQ Sauce (page 38), and top with about 2 tablespoons broken toasted nori seaweed and about 1 teaspoon toasted sesame seeds.

VEGAN SPICY CRAB FRIES: Prepare some Old Bay Mushrooms (page 55). Strip the leaves from about 1 ounce kale (about 1 large leaf), then chop the leaves. Drop the kale into the frying oil until crispy, about 1 minute, then drain on paper towels. Serve the fries with the Vegan Wiz Sauce, Old Bay Mushrooms, fried kale, and a shake of Old Bay seasoning.

At Down North, we squeeze our lemons fresh every morning and keep the juice chilled. Then we mix it with simple syrup to make our different lemonades. People order it at the shop and say, "This is the best lemonade I've ever had!" Ain't no secret to it. Freshness and simplicity are the main ingredients. That goes for the mixers in our other lemonades, too.

We puree fresh strawberries, blueberries, and watermelon for Strawberry Lemonade (page 191), Blueberry Lemonade (page 194), and Watermelon Lemonade (page 198). Cucumber-Mint Lemonade (page 195) is a top seller. If you thought plain lemonade was refreshing, wait 'til you try it with fresh cucumber-mint syrup.

Same thing with the milkshakes. We keep 'em simple. We start with good-quality vanilla ice cream—the kind with the vanilla bean flecks in it—and blitz it with fresh whole milk. Then choose your add-ins. My favorite? Bean Pie Milkshake (page 202). Don't know bean pie? It's a Black American classic. Check the recipe for details.

—MIKE CARTER

THE DOWN NORTH
COMMUNITY
FOUNDATION

My original plan for Down North was Pizza Pi, a nonprofit math-tutoring center to help kids in the neglected Strawberry Mansion neighborhood of North Philly (see page 140). When I pivoted to a pizza restaurant, formerly incarcerated folks became the focus. You can't employ kids in a restaurant, but I wanted to make sure kids remained a part of the Down North mission. That's why I started the nonprofit Down North Foundation: to help divert troubled youth from the preschool-to-prison pipeline.

GROWING FREEDOM AND THE HEALING GARDEN

When young kids make mistakes and break the law, they often go to juvie, the first step in the vast U.S. criminal justice system. At any given time, around 37,000 kids are held in detention centers around the country, and 55 percent of them get rearrested within a year of release. In Philadelphia, the Juvenile Justice Services Center (JJSC) detains about 2,500 boys and girls every year until their criminal cases can be heard. In 2021, we started an urban farm at the JJSC to teach kids about making healthy choices and eating healthy food and to show them what a career in the culinary industry might look like. We call it the Growing Freedom project.

For the project, we have about 3,000 square feet of raised garden beds at the detention center. The kids help us grow all kinds of produce, like watermelons, blueberries, tomatoes, snow peas, sweet peppers, hot peppers, kale, cabbage, carrots, and onions. Since the JJSC is a kind of prison, the Growing Freedom project has been a beacon of light. It gets the kids outside to seed the soil, nurture the plants, and harvest the produce. They also prepare the food, cook it, and eat it. The project's culinary program is led by Mike. Every Tuesday, he teaches the kids valuable cooking skills, and they get a taste of real farm-to-table food. Mike was in this detention center as a kid. It was a different location downtown but the same kind of prison. Mike's biggest goal for the kids is opening their minds to diverse foods and dishes they've never had before.

With Mike's guidance, the youth at JJSC have made things like tortillas from scratch, quick pickles, and empanadas filled with hot peppers and carrots. Mike emphasizes nutrition, teaching them about the health benefits of vegetables, using less salt, using healthier fats like avocado oil, and finding natural sources of sugar, like carrots, instead of turning to white sugar. It's a real cooking class, where everyone learns about nourishing, life-sustaining food. They also get nuggets of wisdom from Mike, who's living proof that turning away from the streets can lead to a successful career.

In March 2023, we also opened a pollinated Healing Garden at JJSC, with medicinal herbs and flowers, a koi fish pond, hammocks, and a gazebo. The Healing Garden provides a tranquil space for kids to begin recovering from the trauma and violence so many of them experience on the streets and at home. It's welcoming for parents, too. Families can visit with each other in the garden and form bonds in a setting that's more conducive to positive change than the inside of a juvenile prison.

In early 2024, we started two other initiatives that support both the Growing Freedom project and the Healing Garden. The 49th Street Greenhouse, a site for seed and plant cultivation, is a place where formerly detained youth extend their agricultural knowledge and skills in paid positions that help them understand the long-term benefits of food sovereignty. Our Restoration Wilderness Therapy program helps to reconnect formerly incarcerated fathers with their children outside the confines of blighted urban neighborhoods. Thus far, more than sixty-five father-child retreats have helped underserved families strengthen their bonds in therapeutic wilderness settings.

DOWN NORTH TREEHOUSE

The Foundation's first initiative stemmed from the Pizza Pi concept. Just down the street from Down North Pizza, there's a big tree on a piece of property that the City of Philadelphia generously donated to the Foundation. That tree inspired the Down North Treehouse, a tech hub that helps prepare school-aged kids for a world dominated by technology. They participate in interactive boot camps on AI, augmented reality, coding, ethical hacking, gaming, graphic design, machine learning, music production, video production, NFTs, cybersecurity, and every other facet of the tech industry. We work with instructors from five different local high schools who teach underprivileged kids in each grade, opening their minds to the possibility of a career in the financially rewarding tech sector.

Like all the Foundation initiatives, the goal of the Treehouse is to divert kids from the preschool-to-prison pipeline. It's hard to visualize that pipeline, but it's real. In urban centers, it's a fact that kids end up on the streets, where they often start entering the street economy and committing crimes. What follows is the juvenile detention center, and then jail, parole, probation, and most often back to jail again. Usually, the cycle begins in the troubled teen years, sometimes when young adults are just starting to have families of their own. The Down North Treehouse is trying to break that vicious cycle by giving kids and young adults employable skills in the tech industry to improve their lives.

PROTECT YA CRIB

Our latest initiative aims to keep adults off the streets by making sure they don't lose their homes. Protect Ya Crib is a program that gives direct financial aid to residents who owe city property taxes. Anyone who owes three or more years of taxes qualifies for the program. We pay their property tax balance up to $5,000, which gives them a clean slate to help them stay on track for the next year's taxes. Residents make small monthly payments into an escrow account, and we match 50 percent of those payments. At the end of the year, the entire balance is available to pay that year's property taxes. We also set it up so residents don't need to do a thing. The Chase Bank pays the city tax collector directly from the escrow account. This initiative helps strengthen our neighborhoods by protecting people from predatory real estate developers and homelessness. It's another way that Down North is trying to improve the lives of residents in underserved communities.

Check out page 206 for ways you can help us fulfill the Down North mission of reducing recidivism in urban centers.

—MUHAMMAD ABDUL-HADI, founder, Down North Pizza

CLASSIC LEMONADE

Right before the grand opening, I was slammed filling out the Down North menu. We had your classic fresh-squeezed lemonade, and then we decided to add other fruit flavors. Every one of the lemonades that follow is refreshing—a little sweet and a little tart. If you have a sweet tooth, you can always up the sugar to taste.

5 cups water

1 cup sugar

2 cups fresh-squeezed and strained lemon juice (from about 13 lemons)

Make a simple syrup by gently simmering the water and the sugar in a medium saucepan over medium heat just until the sugar dissolves, 3 to 4 minutes, stirring once or twice. Remove from the heat and cool completely before using. You can transfer the syrup to a jar or covered container and chill it for several weeks before using, if you want to have it around for lemonade on the fly.

Pour the fresh lemon juice into a 2-quart pitcher and stir in the cold sugar syrup. For each serving, put some ice cubes in a pint glass or cup and pour in 1 to 1½ cups of the lemonade.

DECEMBER 2020 Incarcerated individuals become eligible to apply for Pell grants to fund their college education. All incarcerated individuals become fully eligible for Pell grants on July 1, 2023, nearly thirty years after Pell grant eligibility was revoked through the 1994 Violent Crime and Law Enforcement Act.[118]

STRAWBERRY LEMONADE

**SERVES 4 TO 6
(GENEROUS
1½ QUARTS TOTAL)**

People love pink lemonade. The strawberry flavor is subtle here, but the pink color makes it special. Save this one for the height of strawberry season in early summer, when fresh strawberries taste best.

4 cups water

1 cup sugar

1 quart (about 1½ pounds) strawberries, hulled

2 cups fresh-squeezed and strained lemon juice (from about 13 lemons)

Make the strawberry syrup by gently simmering the water and sugar in a medium saucepan over medium heat just until the sugar dissolves, 3 to 4 minutes, stirring once or twice. Remove from the heat and cool completely.

Put the hulled strawberries into a blender or food processor. Add the cooled syrup and puree until smooth. Use immediately or transfer the syrup to a jar or covered container and chill it for several weeks before using, if you want to have it around for strawberry lemonade on the fly.

Pour the fresh lemon juice into a 1½- to 2-quart pitcher and stir in the cold syrup. For each serving, put some ice cubes in a pint glass or cup and pour in 1 to 1½ cups of the strawberry lemonade.

SEPTEMBER 2021 A report from the Prison Policy Initiative finds that "the U.S. has the highest incarceration rate in the world; every single U.S. state incarcerates more people per capita than virtually any independent democracy on earth."[119]

BLUEBERRY LEMONADE

SERVES
4 TO 6
(GENEROUS
1½ QUARTS
TOTAL)

This is my favorite lemonade. The blueberry flavor is intense, and I love the dark color. Sometimes at the end of a shift, I'll ask Mar to pour me a blueberry. Sometimes I'll add a little tequila, too.

4 cups water

1 cup sugar

1 quart (about 1½ pounds) blueberries, plus some for garnish

2 cups fresh-squeezed and strained lemon juice (from about 13 lemons)

Make the blueberry syrup by gently simmering the water and sugar in a medium saucepan over medium heat just until the sugar dissolves, 3 to 4 minutes, stirring once or twice. Remove from the heat and cool completely.

Put the blueberries in a blender or food processor. Add the cooled syrup and puree until smooth. Use immediately or transfer the syrup to a jar or covered container and chill it for several weeks before using, if you want to have it around for blueberry lemonade on the fly.

Pour the fresh lemon juice into a 1½- to 2-quart pitcher and stir in the cold syrup. For each serving, put some ice cubes in a pint glass or cup and pour in 1 to 1½ cups of the blueberry lemonade. Garnish with fresh blueberries.

MARCH 2, 2023 A widely cited report from the Prison Policy Initiative finds that the carceral system accelerates aging in part due to unhealthy food. Incarcerated individuals lack access to fresh, healthy foods, and their diets consist of highly processed, sugary foods that contribute to poor health outcomes and chronic health conditions. Food, or lack thereof, is also used as a form of punishment during incarceration.[120,121,122,123]

CUCUMBER-MINT LEMONADE

SERVES 4 TO 6 (GENEROUS 1½ QUARTS TOTAL)

When the cucumber plants start flowing, I pickle the cucumbers. One time I didn't have enough pickling jars for them all, and I had some fresh mint. I started dreaming of a mojito-type situation. I threw the cukes and mint into a blender, and now Cucumber-Mint Lemonade is one of our all-time best-selling drinks. Add a shot of rum for that mojito taste.

4 cups water

1 cup sugar

1 cup loosely packed fresh mint leaves (about 1 ounce), plus a couple of sprigs for garnish

3 English cucumbers (about 1½ pounds), ends trimmed, coarsely chopped, plus some cucumber slices for garnish

2 cups fresh-squeezed and strained lemon juice (from about 13 lemons)

Cucumber slices and fresh mint sprigs for garnish (optional)

Make the cucumber-mint syrup by gently simmering the water and sugar in a medium saucepan over medium heat just until the sugar dissolves, 3 to 4 minutes, stirring once or twice. Remove from the heat and cool completely.

To ensure your mint stays bright green, set up a small pot of boiling water and a small bowl of ice water. Dunk the mint leaves into the boiling water and cook until bright green, about 30 seconds. Then use a slotted spoon to transfer the mint to the ice water to stop the cooking. Drain on paper towels to dry.

When the mint leaves have cooled, transfer the mint to a blender or food processor. Add the cucumbers and cooled syrup, and puree until smooth. Use immediately, or transfer the syrup to a jar or covered container and chill it for several weeks before using, if you want to have it around for cucumber-mint lemonade on the fly.

Pour the fresh lemon juice into a 1½- to 2-quart pitcher and stir in the cold syrup. For each serving, put some ice cubes in a pint glass or cup and pour in 1 to 1½ cups of the cucumber-mint lemonade. Garnish with a cucumber wheel and fresh mint sprig for a little glow up.

AUGUST 15, 2023 A *New York Times* investigation finds that "Philadelphia, with less than 1 percent of the country's population, accounted for more than 10 percent of all children sentenced to life in prison without parole."[124] Begun in the 1980s, the practice of incarcerating youth for life continued until 2012, when the U.S. Supreme Court declared life sentences for youth unconstitutional.[125]

WATERMEL

A Quaker friend of ours, Neil, is a farmer who lives in the countryside outside Philadelphia. When he comes into the city to attend Quaker meetings, he brings us produce. One time in the summer, he brought a load of watermelons and we needed to use it all up before the fruit flies got to it. We cut it up and made watermelon lemonade. For this one, we like to add a little slice of watermelon rind to the cup for a pop of green color.

4 cups water

1 cup sugar

4 cups (about 1½ pounds) chopped fresh seedless watermelon, plus the rind for garnish

2 cups fresh-squeezed and strained lemon juice (from about 13 lemons)

Make the watermelon syrup by gently simmering the water and sugar in a medium saucepan over medium heat just until the sugar dissolves, 3 to 4 minutes, stirring once or twice. Remove from the heat and cool completely.

Put the chopped watermelon in a blender or food processor. Add the cooled syrup and puree until smooth. Use immediately or transfer the syrup to a jar or covered container and chill it for several weeks before using, if you want to have it around for watermelon lemonade on the fly.

Pour the fresh lemon juice into a 1½- to 2-quart pitcher and stir in the cold syrup. For each serving, put some ice cubes in a pint glass or cup and pour in 1 to 1½ cups of the watermelon lemonade. Garnish with a small wedge of watermelon, including the rind.

OCTOBER 11, 2023 The Sentencing Project finds that "one in five Black men born in 2001 is likely to experience imprisonment within their lifetime, a decline from one in three for those born in 1981."[126]

ON LEMONADE

VANILLA MILKSHAKE

Muhammad's sister, Wadiya Gooden, is a chef, and she makes her own vanilla extract by curing vanilla beans in bourbon. Most people don't go to those lengths to make a vanilla milkshake, so for this recipe just pick up some good-quality vanilla bean ice cream, the kind with the flecks in it.

As any ice cream lover knows, the add-ins are where it's at. One of our favorites is the Bean Pie Milkshake. If you're not familiar, bean pie is a creamy custard pie similar to sweet potato pie but made with pureed navy beans. It's an iconic symbol of Black Muslim power, referenced in rap songs, TV shows, and street murals. Look for it online and at Black Muslim bakeries. We get ours from Ali Bean Pie in Philadelphia.

3 scoops (about 1½ cups) real vanilla bean ice cream, slightly softened

About ½ cup whole milk

Whipped cream (optional)

Chill a pint glass in the freezer while you're softening up your ice cream. Puree the softened ice cream and milk in a blender until creamy and smooth. You can also use a stick blender and tall quart container. Pour into the chilled glass, top with whipped cream (if using), and serve with a fat straw.

remix

VEGAN VANILLA MILKSHAKE: Use plant-based vanilla ice cream, extra-creamy oat milk, and vegan whipped cream (if using).

STRAWBERRY MILKSHAKE: Add 5 to 6 tablespoons strawberry syrup (see page 191) along with the ice cream and milk.

OREO MILKSHAKE: After blending the ice cream and milk, quickly blend in ¼ to ⅓ cup crushed Oreo cookie pieces (2 to 3 cookies), until the shake has a cookies 'n cream look to it. For a garnish, crush some Oreo cookies to dust and sprinkle the Oreo dust over your whipped cream (if using).

APPLE PIE MILKSHAKE: Pour a 21-ounce can of apple pie filling, 2 tablespoons ground cinnamon, and ½ cup caramel sauce (the kind you spoon over ice cream) into a blender. Blend until smooth, then add 5 to 6 tablespoons of apple pie seasoning along with the ice cream and milk for your shake. A plus up: Make a caramel swirl inside the glass. Spoon some caramel sauce around the inside top of your milkshake glass, tilting the glass as you go. Top with whipped cream (if using) and add a sprinkle of cinnamon sugar. Looks fire!

BEAN PIE MILKSHAKE: Blend in some bean pie along with the ice cream and milk. We buy the 6-inch bean pies, quarter 'em, and toss in 1 pie quarter per milkshake.

NOVEMBER 25, 2023 The *New York Times* publishes a map that illustrates how 42 years of marijuana arrests disproportionately ensnared Black and Latinx people for decades.[127]

HOW YOU CAN HELP

All the Down North Foundation initiatives help to fulfill the Down North mission of reducing recidivism in urban centers. Any net proceeds Muhammad earns from the sale of this book will be donated to the Down North Foundation. Thank you for your support! Donations can also be made at the Foundation website: **https://www.downnorthfoundation.org/.**

The United States has the highest incarceration rate in the world, with over 2 million people in jails and prisons. We also have the highest recidivism rate, with 70 percent of prisoners returning to jail within five years of release. Black men account for most of these numbers: one in three will be imprisoned in his lifetime, and 72 percent will return to prison within three years.

When you look at it all as a whole, Down North is tackling some massive issues: a troubled criminal justice system, widening economic inequality, neglected inner-city infrastructure, and structural racism. We're just one small pizza shop trying to address these big issues and give formerly incarcerated men and women a second chance in life. If you're able to help, here's what else you can do in addition to buying our pizza and donating to the Foundation.

ADVOCATE FOR CRIMINAL JUSTICE REFORM

Achieving fairness, equity, and true rehabilitation in our justice system requires proactive policy changes. You can help by supporting policies such as sentencing reform, alternatives to incarceration, and diversion programs that provide rehabilitation opportunities rather than punishment. People often get involved with the system because they don't have access to the resources and support they need to thrive. You can help reduce mass incarceration in your community by supporting policies, programs, and organizations that aim to uplift those in need so they don't end up behind bars. Show your support by voting, donating, or volunteering your time.

SUPPORT ACCESS TO EDUCATION

It's no secret that higher education can lead to better employment opportunities. Support initiatives that increase access to vocational training, job skills development, and higher education, both during incarceration and after release.

PROMOTE EMPLOYMENT OPPORTUNITIES

Employment is critical for returning citizens to successfully reintegrate into their communities. Advocate for policies that remove employment barriers for those with a criminal record, such as "ban the box" laws that prohibit employers from asking about criminal history on job applications. Support initiatives that provide job training, job placement, and entrepreneurship opportunities for formerly incarcerated individuals. If you are in the position to do so, support equitable hiring practices at your own workplace.

ADDRESS RACIAL DISPARITIES

Black people have a higher incarceration rate than any other racial group in the United States. Advocate for addressing structural racism in the criminal justice system, including biases in policing, prosecution, and sentencing. Support initiatives that promote racial equity and diversity. For more details about systemic racism, see the U.S. Incarceration System Timeline woven throughout this book.

SUPPORT MENTAL HEALTH AND SUBSTANCE ABUSE TREATMENT PROGRAMS

Black men are disproportionately impacted by substance abuse and mental health issues. Advocate for access to quality mental health resources and substance abuse treatment that addresses the unique needs of African American men both during incarceration and after release.

PROVIDE COMMUNITY SUPPORT

When someone is struggling, a strong local network can be a lifeline. In your community, get behind initiatives that provide counseling, mentoring, positive relationships, and social support to help prevent formerly incarcerated individuals from reoffending.

PROMOTE FAMILY REUNIFICATION

Incarceration can wreak havoc on families. Support policies and programs that promote family reunification, such as visitation programs, family therapy, and support for maintaining family connections during incarceration. Strong family support can be a protective factor against recidivism.

—MUHAMMAD ABDUL-HADI

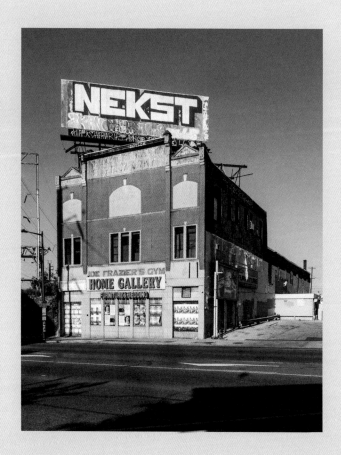

FRIENDS OF DOWN NORTH

Down North Pizza and the Down North Foundation are fortunate to work with supportive partners in Philadelphia, around the United States, and around the world. Our partners are instrumental in furthering the Down North mission of restructuring relation-ships, culture, and places to reduce recidivism rates in urban communities.

SCHOLARS

Ajima Olaghere

Ajima Olaghere, PhD, is a social entrepreneur and former assistant professor of criminal justice at Temple University in Philadelphia, where she pursued community-engaged research and lectured on topics such as re-entry, the social determinants of crime, the intersection of crime and social policy, and data equity. She is an aspiring urban gardener and long-time partner/advocate of the Down North Foundation, where she serves as strategic advisor.

Celeste Winston

Celeste Winston, PhD, is an abolitionist geographer and assistant professor of geography and urban studies at Temple University. Her work centers everyday Black life and placemaking practices as models for liberation. She aims to generate evidence for more livable and equitable geographies by tracing the legacies of Black alternative ways of living and building communities across space and time. Her first book

How to Lose the Hounds: Maroon Geographies and a World Beyond Policing, was published by Duke University Press in 2023, and she is part of the Down North Foundation leadership team.

Sami Atif

Sami Atif, PhD, is director of equity and inclusion at the Fessenden School in Newtown, Massachusetts, and adjunct professor in mathematics at Bentley University in Waltham, Massachusetts. As a published mathematician and equity consultant, his work leverages data and narrative to improve the lives of the historically marginalized. He shares his expertise with the Down North Foundation as a consultant.

CHEFS

Marc Vetri

Marc Vetri is the chef and founder of the critically acclaimed Vetri Cucina, Fiorella, and Pizzeria Salvy in Philadelphia; Vetri Cucina Las Vegas, Fiorella Las Vegas, and Osteria Fiorella in Vegas; and Mr. Maurice's Italian in Kyoto, Japan. A Philadelphia

native, Marc is the author of five cookbooks and the driving force behind the Vetri Community Partnership, a nonprofit dedicated to nutrition education. Check out his collab pizza recipe on page 144.

Michael Solomonov

Mike Solomonov is chef of the trailblazing Israeli restaurant Zahav and co-owner of Philadelphia's CookNSolo Restaurants with hospitality entrepreneur Steve Cook. The CookNSolo portfolio also features Federal Donuts, Dizengoff, Goldie, K'Far, Laser Wolf, and Lilah. CookNSolo expanded to Brooklyn bringing Laser Wolf, K'Far, and Jaffa Cocktail & Raw Bar to The Hoxton hotel. Together, Mike and Steve have authored three highly acclaimed cookbooks. Check out his collab pizza recipe on page 148.

Shenarri Freeman

Shenarri Freeman is the executive chef of the vegan soul food restaurant Cadence in New York City and the plant-based West African–inspired Ubuntu in Los Angeles. She has been nominated for two James

Beard Foundation Awards and is a *Forbes* "30 Under 30" recipient. Check out her collab pizza recipe on page 152.

Marcus Samuelsson
Marcus Samuelsson is the renowned chef behind Hav & Mar, Red Rooster, and Metropolis in New York City, as well as Overtown in Miami and several MARCUS locations in the Bahamas, Newark, and Atlanta. He has won eight James Beard Foundation Awards and is a longstanding judge on the Food Network show *Chopped* as well as the author of several acclaimed cookbooks and a bestselling memoir. Marcus also cochairs Careers Through Culinary Arts Program (C-CAP), a thirty-four-year-old nonprofit organization that furthers social justice by preparing underserved youth and formerly incarcerated individuals for careers in the culinary industry. Check out his collab pizza recipe on page 155.

Reem Assil
Reem Assil is the chef-activist of the acclaimed

Reem's California, a modern Arab street corner bakery in San Francisco. She is also the author of the award-winning *Arabiyya: Recipes from the Life of an Arab in Diaspora*. Working at the intersection of food, community, and social justice, Reem uses Arab hospitality to build a strong, resilient community. Check out her collab pizza recipe on page 158.

Nicole and Michael Nicholas
Nicole and Michael Nicholas are the proprietors of Aunts et Uncles, a vegan café in the Little Caribbean district of Brooklyn, New York. The café serves as a hub for Caribbean food, music, and art in the community. Check out their collab pizza recipe on page 160.

Cristina Martinez
Cristina Martinez is the James Beard Award–winning chef of South Philly Barbacoa and Casa Mexico. Cristina was raised in Mexico by barbacoa masters and along with her husband, Benjamin Miller, she contributes to the People's Kitchen at El

Compadre in Philadelphia, which serves free meals to those in need.

Randy Rucker
Randy Rucker is chef-owner of Philadelphia's River Twice restaurant and has been nominated for multiple James Beard Awards.

COMMUNICATIONS

Natasha Gullett
Natasha Gullett is a communications and brand executive with more than twenty years of experience. She has spent her career launching new brands and products, working alongside passionate and innovative teams. A large part of her career was spent in hospitality, most notably leading the InterContinental Hotels Group consumer public relations practice for nearly a decade. In addition to her work with Down North Pizza, Natasha balances consulting projects and entrepreneurship. Currently, she spends her time traveling throughout Mexico, waiting for Down North Pizza to launch there.

Kirkland Lynch
Kirkland Lynch is the chief executive officer at Barking Owl, a four-time winner of *Ad Age*'s Music and Sound Company of the Year. He focuses on music sound design and mixing for the commercial advertising industry and beyond, including sonic branding and mnemonics for *Fortune* 500 and blue chip brands.

The Working Remotely
The Working Remotely is a private, global, digital networking and lifestyle community of thought-leaders, professionals, and culture changers exchanging expert advice and tools to uplevel their skillset. Founded in 2018 and headquartered in Los Angeles, the community promotes a world where we don't have to sacrifice personal dreams for professional advancement.

PHILADELPHIA PARTNERS

Jack O'Brien
John J. "Jack" O'Brien is a partner in the investment management practice in

the Philadelphia office of the law firm Morgan Lewis. He counsels registered and private funds and fund managers in connection with organizational, offering, transactional, and compliance matters. As a whole, the Morgan Lewis law firm provides high-quality litigation, corporate, labor and employment, and intellectual property services to clients across industry sectors and regions around the world.

Heather Leach

Heather Leach is an ethnobotanist who utilizes her skills in education and agriculture to support and promote community-based initiatives to protect and conserve local cultures and environments, particularly in the areas of Indigenous food sovereignty and underserved communities. Through a contract with the Philadelphia Department of Prisons, she manages the Philadelphia Prison Orchard and works with inmates in paid positions to prepare them for agriculture-related jobs.

Triple Bottom Brewing

Triple Bottom Brewing is a Philadelphia craft brewery and certified B corp with a triple bottom line: beer, people, and the planet. The brewery is powered by renewable energy and fair chance practices, actively hiring people who may otherwise be excluded from the mainstream economy, including people who have experienced homelessness or incarceration.

Friends of the Wissahickon

Friends of the Wissahickon (FOW) is a nonprofit organization that conserves, stewards, and advocates for the 2,000 acres of Philadelphia's Wissahickon Valley Park. Its mission is to conserve the natural beauty and wildness of the Wissahickon Valley and stimulate public interest in it. With more than 3,000 members, FOW works in partnership with the Philadelphia Parks & Recreation Department, the Philadelphia Water Department, and dozens of other regional partners on a wide range

of programs, including watershed education, trail maintenance, and park user safety. In 2024, FOW celebrated its 100th year of stewardship for the Wissahickon park, a centerpiece for recreation for the greater Philadelphia area.

Eastern State Penitentiary

Eastern State Penitentiary is the world's first true penitentiary and a U.S. National Historic Landmark in Philadelphia. It was operational from 1829 to 1971 and is currently open to the public for tours. Down North serves pizza at the penitentiary to further its message of prison reform and its mission of reducing recidivism in underserved inner-city communities.

Juvenile Justice Services Center

The Juvenile Justice Services Center (JJSC) is a secure juvenile detention facility that houses youth, both male and female, between the ages of 13 to 20 who have been ordered to be held there by the Philadelphia

courts. The 184-bed facility accommodates about 2,500 youth annually, and residents receive on-site education by the School District of Philadelphia. Residents also have access to physical and behavioral health services, recreational programming, social work services, religious programming, and an array of other supplemental services and programs. Down North's Growing Freedom Project is a 3,000-square-foot urban farm at JJSC that teaches kids about making healthy choices, eating healthy food, and potential careers in the culinary industry. Down North also operates the Healing Garden at JJSC, which provides a tranquil space outside the juvenile prison for kids to begin recovering from the trauma and violence experienced on the streets and at home.

U.S. INCARCERATION SYSTEM TIMELINE NOTES

For further reading, here are sources for the U.S. incarceration system timeline that appears throughout this book.

1 Bureau of Justice Statistics, "Probation and Parole in the United States, 2021," Prisons Report Series: Preliminary Data Release and Jails Report Series: Preliminary Data Release.

2 https://criticalresistance.org/resources/policing-timeline/

3 https://jimcrowmuseum.ferris.edu/timeline/slavery.htm

4 Ibid.

5 https://criticalresistance.org/resources/policing-timeline/

6 https://encyclopediavirginia.org/entries/servant-and-slave-patrols-in-virginia/

7 https://constitutioncenter.org/the-constitution/historic-document-library/detail/the-fugitive-slave-act-1850

8 https://www.blackpast.org/african-american-history/events-african-american-history/the-bridge-biddy-mason-case-1856/

9 https://www.pbs.org/wgbh/aia/part4/4p2932.html

10 https://nmaach.si.edu/explore/stories/historical-legacy-juneteenth

11 https://blogs.loc.gov/inside_adams/2021/06/convict-leasing-system/

12 https://eji.org/news/history-racial-injustice-convict-leasing/

13 https://www.pbs.org/wnet/african-americans-many-riversto-cross/history/the-truth-behind-40-acres-and-a-mule/

14 https://chroniclingamerica.loc.gov/lccn/sn84021918/1961-10-13/ed-1/seq-2/

15 https://www.archives.gov/research/african-americans/freedmens-bureau

16 https://eji.org/report/reconstruction-in-america/

17 https://eji.org/news/history-racial-injustice-sharecropping/

18 https://texancultures.utsa.edu/cabin/history/

19 https://www.vera.org/reimagining-prison-web-report/american-history-race-and-prison

20 https://eji.org/reports/lynching-in-america/

21 https://criticalresistance.org/resources/policing-timeline/

22 https://www.blackpast.org/african-american-history/wysinger-v-crookshank-1888/

23 https://www.blackpast.org/african-american-history/plessy-v-ferguson-1896-0/

24 https://www.archives.gov/milestone-documents/plessy-v-ferguson

25 https://criticalresistance.org/resources/policing-timeline/

26 https://www.archives.gov/research/african-americans/migrations/great-migration

27 https://scholarshare.temple.edu/handle/20.500.12613/7497

28 https://eji.org/news/history-racial-injustice-red-summer-of-1919/

29 https://www.blackpast.org/african-american-history/omaha-courthouse-lynching-1919/

30 https://www.justsecurity.org/76699/reckoning-with-state-sanctioned-racial-violence-lessons-from-the-tulsa-race-massacre/

31 https://www.blackpast.org/african-american-history/tulsa-race-riot-1921/

32 https://www.neh.gov/article/1921-tulsa-massacre

33 https://www.blackpast.org/african-american-history/scottsboro-boys-trial-and-defense-campaign-1931-1937/

34 https://criticalresistance.org/resources/policing-timeline/

35 Ibid.

36 Ibid.

37 https://www.pbs.org/hueypnewton/actions/actions_cointelpro.html

38 https://criticalresistance.org/resources/policing-timeline/

39 https://snccdigital.org/events/fannie-lou-hamer-founds-freedom-farm-cooperative/

40 https://www.womenofthehall.org/inductee/fannie-lou-hamer/

41 https://kinginstitute.stanford.edu/hamer-fannie-lou

42 https://snccdigital.org/people/fannie-lou-hamer/

43 https://www.archives.gov/research/african-americans/vote/freedom-summer

44 https://www.blackpast.org/african-american-history/freedom-summer-1964/

45 https://www.blackpast.org/african-american-history/bloody-sunday-selma-alabama-march-7-1965/

46 https://criticalresistance.org/resources/policing-timeline/

47 Ibid.

48 https://nmaahc.si.edu/explore/stories/kerner-commission

49 https://criticalresistance.org/resources/policing-timeline

50 https://libguides.mnhs.org/aim

51 https://criticalresistance.org/materials/the-first-rainbow-coalition/

52 Ibid.

53 https://www.zinnedproject.org/materials/the-first-rainbow-coalition/

54 https://www.blackpast.org/african-american-history/blackpanther-partys-free-breakfastprogram-1969-1980/

55 https://www.theguardian.com/us-news/2019/oct/17/blackpanther-party-oakland-free-breakfast-50th-anniversary

56 https://www.vera.org/news/fifty-years-ago-today-president-nixon-declared-the-war-on-drugs

57 https://drugpolicy.org/drug-war-history/

58 https://time.com/6090016/us-war-on-drugs-origins/

59 Ibid.

60 https://www.blackpast.org/african-american-history/attica-prison-riot-1971-2/

61 https://www.npr.org/2021/10/27/1049295683/attica-prison-documentary-stanley-nelson

62 https://criticalresistance.org/resources/policing-timeline/

63 Ibid.

64 https://belonging.berkeley.edu/new-southern-strategy

65 https://drugpolicy.org/drug-war-history/

66 https://www.congress.gov/bill/98th-congress/senate-bill/1762

67 https://www.congress.gov/bill/100th-congress/house-bill/5210

68 https://www.aclu.org/press-releases/aclu-releases-crack-cocaine-report-anti-drug-abuse-act-1986-deepened-racial-inequity

69 https://www.congress.gov/bill/98th-congress/house-bill/5773

70 https://www.ussc.gov/research/research-and-publications/simplification-draft-paper-2

71 https://stoprecidivism.org/recidivism/the-history-behind-mandatory-minimums/

72 https://www.blackpast.org/african-american-history/events-african-american-history/move-bombing-1985/

73 https://www.aclu.org/issues/criminal-law-reform/fair-sentencing-act

74 https://www.blackpast.org/african-american-history/central-park-five-1989/

75 https://apnews.com/article/new-york-city-council-election-yusef-salaam-0377cedcbd29f-424753c9790551a85de

76 https://www.vox.com/2015/2/24/8101289/school-discipline-race

77 https://www.aclu.org/documents/what-school-prison-pipeline

78 https://eji.org/news/superpredator-myth-20-years-later/

79 https://www.sagepub.com/sites/default/files/upm-binaries/27206_1.pdf

80 https://www.sentencingproject.org/reports/mass-incarceration-trends/

81 https://www.nytimes.com/2019/06/25/us/joe-biden-crime-laws.html

82 https://criticalresistance.org/resources/policing-timeline/

83 https://www.prisonpolicy.org/blog/2019/08/22/college-in-prison/

84 https://eji.org/news/history-racial-injustice-felony-disenfranchisement/

85 https://www.sentencingproject.org/reports/dispropor-tionate-minority-contact-in-the-juvenile-justice-system/

86 https://jacobin.com/2015/05/stop-and-frisk-dragnet-ferguson-baltimore/

87 https://www.americanbar.org/groups/criminal_justice/publications/criminal-justice-magazine/2020/winter/racial-profiling-past-present-and-future/

88 https://www.sentencingproject.org/reports/report-to-the-united-nations-on-racial-disparities-in-the-u-s-criminal-justice-system/#footnote-5

89 https://criticalresistance.org/resources/policing-timeline/

90 https://www.aclu.org/issues/national-security/privacy-and-surveillance/surveillance-under-patriot-act

91 https://www.urban.org/sites/default/files/publication/60721/410633-Criminal-Justice-and-Health-and-Human-Services.PDF

92 https://milliondollarhoods.pre.ss.ucla.edu/about-us/

93 https://www.npr.org/2012/10/02/162149431/million-dollar-blocks-map-incarcerations-costs

94 https://www.umass.edu/news/article/new-study-finds-black-adults-us-are-more-likely-have-had-more-family-members

95 https://www.theatlantic.com/magazine/archive/2015/10/the-black-family-in-the-age-of-mass-incarceration/403246/

96 https://www.blackpast.org/african-american-history/events-african-american-history/jena-six-2006/

97 https://thenewpress.com/books/mass-supervision

98 https://www.hrw.org/report/2020/07/31/revoked/how-probation-and-parole-feed-mass-incarceration-united-states

99 https://www.theatlantic.com/politics/archive/2019/12/parole-mass-supervision-crisis/604108/

100 https://www.sentencingproject.org/advocacy/50-years-and-a-wake-up-ending-the-mass-incarceration-crisis-in-america/

101 https://nicic.gov/weblink/too-big-succeed-impact-growth-community-corrections-and-what-should-be-done-about-it

102 https://criticalresistance.org/resources/policing-timeline/

103 https://www.nilc.org/issues/immigration-enforcement/along-racial-lines-arizonas-sb1070/

104 https://www.aclu.org/sb-1070-supreme-court-whats-stake

105 https://www.azleg.gov/legtext/49leg/2r/bills/sb1070s.pdf

106 https://www.aclu.org/issues/criminal-law-reform/fair-sentencing-act?redirect=issues/criminal-law-reform/drug-law-reform/fair-sentencing-act

107 https://www.brennancenter.org/our-work/analysis-opinion/thousands-prisoners-now-eligi-ble-receive-fairer-sentences

108 https://www.apa
.org/monitor/2014/10/
incarceration

109 https://criticalresistance
.org/resources/policing-timeline/

110 Ibid.

111 https://americanindian
.si.edu/nk360/plains-treaties/dapl

112 https://criticalresistance.org/
resources/policing-timeline/

113 https://www.apha.org/
policies-and-advocacy/public-
health-policy-statements/policy-
database/2019/01/29/
law-enforcement-violence

114 https://www.metrowest
dailynews.com/story/opinion/
columns/2019/08/28/
immediate-changes-needed-in-
criminal/4365975007/

115 https://www.aclu.org/news/
immigrants-rights/the-enduring-
harms-of-trumps-muslim-ban

116 https://criticalresistance.org/
resources/policing-timeline/

117 https://www.npr.
org/2023/11/13/1210564359/
slavery-prison-forced-labor-
movement

118 https://www.vera.org/news-
room/vera-celebrates-historic-
pell-reinstatement

119 https://www.prisonpolicy
.org/global/2021.html

120 https://www.thedailymeal
.com/1213267/what-prison-food-
is-really-like-around-the-united-
states/

121 https://www.annualreviews
.org/doi/full/10.1146/annurev-
publhealth-071521-034016

122 https://www.prison
policy.org/blog/2023/08/02/aging

123 https://www.theguardian
.com/society/2018/oct/16/
prisoners-age-more-quickly-than-
general-population-inspectors-say

124 https://www.nytimes
.com/2023/08/15/headway/
prison-life-sentence-release.html

125 https://www.sentencing
project.org/reports/slow-to-act-
state-responses-to-2012-
supreme-court-mandate-on-life-
without-parole/

126 https://www.sentencing
project.org/reports/one-in-five-
ending-racial-inequity-in-
incarceration/

127 https://www.nytimes
.com/2023/11/24/nyregion/
marijuana-legal-arrests-ny-race
.html

ACKNOWLEDGMENTS

FROM MUHAMMAD ABDUL-HADI

I have so many people to thank, including Dope Botanicals (Taahirah Stith and Nakia Stith), Natasha Gullett, Adam McFarland, Marliesse Stevenson, Jameel Bridgewater, Lucy Edosmwan, Kiara Moreno, Imani Briscoe, Brandi McLaughlin (the attorney who worked my case), Kirkland Lynch (my childhood friend, thanks for believing in Down North from the first day I told you about the idea), Shenarri Freeman, Camari Mick, Brittney Williams, Rasheeda Purdie, Nahna Willont, Jaz Johnson, Lana Lagomarsini, Jeanette Maldonado, Randy Rucker, Mike and Nicole Nicolas from Aunts et Uncles, all my chef friends' friends, Dr. Brian Sims, Dr. Vanya Jones, the entire Down North Foundation team, including Dr. Sami Atif, Dr. Ajima Olaghere, Dr. Celeste Winston, Dr. Talia Lesane, Heather Leach, Makayla Myers, Devin Uqdah, Cydney Preston, Simone King, Taalib Din, Shuja Moore, and Jeff Dowana and Chloe Perry (who tasted the first-ever Down North Pizza), as well as Tremayne Lipscomb, Desire Levy-Vincent, Dr. Kimberly McGlonn, Lisa Servon, Albert Brady, Jermaine McMihelk, Scott Morris, Cardell Davis, Jason Okonkwo, Amiyr Muhammad, Christa Barfield (FarmerJawn), Momin Sheikh, Latifa Uqdah, Mansoor Abdul-Hadi, Munir Abdul-Hadi, Masud Abdul-Hadi, iKraam Abdul-Hadi, Tyree Dancey, Kevin Tilery, Nina Noel, Michael Carter, Jamar Johnson, Derrick Cobb, Amurri Kinsey, David Joachim, Raquel Pelzel, Sally Ekus, the entire Down North family, Currant Swint and the KRT Team and, especially, everyone incarcerated in America.

FROM MICHAEL CARTER

This is all still surreal because I remember my first convo with Muhammad about writing a cookbook. It was the Heads of the Table dinner for *Bon Appétit*. That night I met the restaurateur Simon Kim; Anna Wintour from *Vogue* was there; and I met revolutionary-chef Reem Assil, whose collab pie you can check out in this book. I met plenty of other amazing trailblazers in the industry. The most important was Dawn Davis. She even sat me next to Marcus Samuelsson and said I needed to know him. So big shout-out to Dawn for connecting the dots that outlined this awesome book's inception.

I scrambled for months getting the recipes together for Dave to edit and test. Never knew how laborious it would be. Or how satisfying it would be to finally hear two words: "We're done." It was pure hustle and sweat opening Down North, so I relish the opportunity to rewind and walk down memory lane. Big thanx to Muhammad for giving me the keys and trusting that I could get us here more than five years ago. I can't forget my guys: Mar, thanx for the early mornings making three hundred-plus doughs when the lines were down to 29th Street. You saved me from early burnout. Thanx to D-Nice and Kassem for rocking out every shift. Thanx to my former staff and all my friends that have volunteered and held us down. Dom and Mel (P.I.T.P.)—big shout-out to the constant flow of influencers and foodies that continue to help us spread the Down North gospel.

Lastly, I'd like to thank my family for being flexible babysitters because you knew I was chasing a dream, and for all the endless support you've given, and the popups and pizza tests you've endured: Mom, Tory, Milan, Anna Banana, E, Ray, Lay, Ju, Cell, EJ, Kristin, Naj, Ruby, Maasai, and Lulu. A.P.I.D.T.A., the best of planners.

FROM DAVID JOACHIM

Thank you Sally Ekus for bringing Muhammad and me together. As always, you've been a not-so-secret agent extraordinaire throughout this project. Muhammad, major props for entrusting your story and this cookbook to me, a white dude who lives outside the city. That was a leap of faith! It's been pure pleasure getting to know you and shepherding your vision and heart of gold to these pages. Mike, I so enjoyed our cooking visits and conversations, and I'm sad they've come to an end! Same goes for Mar, Derrick, Myles, Perm, Miss Tremelle, and everyone else at Down North Pizza. Thank you for letting me tell your stories. Let's do another book! Big thanks to the chefs who collaborated with Down North and contributed recipes to this book, including Marcus Samuelsson, Shenarri Freeman, Reem Assil, Marc Vetri, Mike Solomonov, and Nicole and Michael Nicholas. Your pizzas are all knockouts. Hugs to the taste testers throughout recipe testing, especially Christine, August, and Maddox, who never groaned at yet another pizza night. And to Ajima, a huge thank-you for your diligent research for the Preface and the timeline of the U.S. incarceration system that appears on nearly every page of this book. That information has been critical in fulfilling our collective vision for this being much more than a book of great recipes and stories. To Amurri, your stunning photographs have done more to bring this book to life than I ever could have imagined. I wish Covid hadn't kept me from the pizza photoshoots! At Clarkson Potter, thank you Raquel for your steady editorial hand, guiding this book from proposal to printed page and letting it be a little different than most Potter cookbooks. To Stephanie Huntwork, nice work on the book design—it's a stunner! Thanks also to the rest of the Potter team, including Elaine Hennig, Alex Noya, Jessica Heim, and Abby Oladipo, for catching errant mistakes, keeping us on schedule, and getting the word out about this one-of-a-kind cookbook. As this project makes abundantly clear, it takes a village to get anything important done in this world, whether that's making a unique, mission-driven cookbook or reforming a troubled prison system.

INDEX

Note: Page references in *italics* indicate photographs.

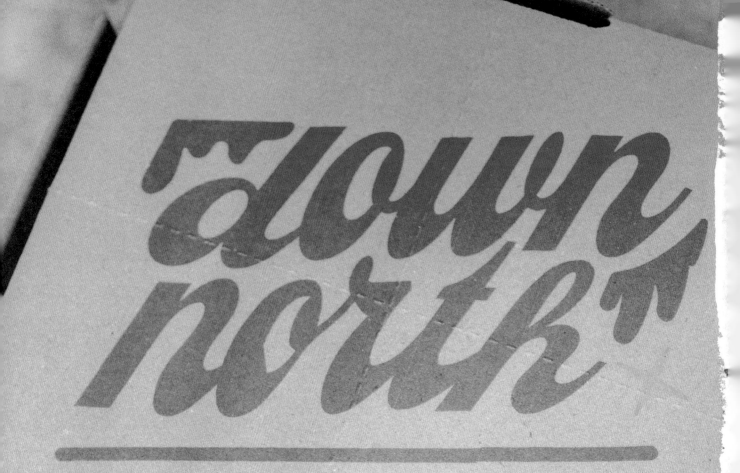

Published in the United States by Clarkson Potter/Publishers, an imprint of the Crown Publishing Group, a division of Penguin Random House LLC, New York. ClarksonPotter.com

Library of Congress Cataloging-in-Publication Data is available upon request at https://lccn.loc.gov/2024011091

ISBN 978-0-593-79640-5
Ebook ISBN 978-0-593-79641-2

Printed in China

Editor: Raquel Pelzel | Editorial assistant: Elaine Hennig
Designer: Stephanie Huntwork
Production editor: Abby Oladipo
Production manager: Jessica Heim
Compositors: Merri Ann Morrell and Hannah Hunt
Food stylist: Michael Carter
Food stylist assistant: Muhammad Abdul-Hadi
Prop stylist: Amurri Lauren
Prop stylist assistant: Muhammad Abdul-Hadi
Photo assistant: Muhammad Abdul-Hadi
Photo retoucher: Amurri Lauren
Recipe developer: Michael Carter
Recipe tester: David Joachim
Copyeditor: Carole Berglie
Proofreaders: Hope Clarke and Penny Haynes | Indexer: Elizabeth Parson
Publicist: Felix Cruz | Marketer: Joey Lozada

10 9 8 7 6 5 4 3 2 1

First Edition